George & Donita—
It is a privilege
to work for you.

*[signature]*
2/21/2019

# TRANSFORMATIONAL INVESTING

TOM HALVORSON

J. RICHARD COE

# TRANSFORMATIONAL
# INVESTING

*How To Have More for What Matters Through a*
**Transformational Approach to Investing**

Published by Advantage, Charleston, South Carolina.
Member of Advantage Media Group.

ADVANTAGE is a registered trademark, and the Advantage colophon is a trademark of Advantage Media Group, Inc.

Printed in the United States of America.

10  9  8  7  6  5  4  3  2  1

ISBN: 978-1-59932-911-6
LCCN: 2018962237

Cover design by George Stevens.
Layout design by Megan Elger.

This publication is designed to provide accurate and authoritative information in regard to the subject matter covered. It is sold with the understanding that the publisher is not engaged in rendering legal, accounting, or other professional services. If legal advice or other expert assistance is required, the services of a competent professional person should be sought.

Advantage Media Group is proud to be a part of the Tree Neutral® program. Tree Neutral offsets the number of trees consumed in the production and printing of this book by taking proactive steps such as planting trees in direct proportion to the number of trees used to print books. To learn more about Tree Neutral, please visit **www.treeneutral.com**.

Advantage Media Group is a publisher of business, self-improvement, and professional development books and online learning. We help entrepreneurs, business leaders, and professionals share their Stories, Passion, and Knowledge to help others Learn & Grow. Do you have a manuscript or book idea that you would like us to consider for publishing? Please visit **advantagefamily.com** or call **1.866.775.1696**.

*This book is dedicated to those who matter most to me: Cheryl, my wife and life companion these past forty-four years; Kendra; Lauren; Nathan; and Spencer; our awesome daughters and sons-in-law; and of course, our beautiful grandchildren, Everly and Harrison.*

—Tom Halvorson

*To Deb Coe, my wife since 1982, mother of our sons David and Doug, grandmother to our grandchildren, my best friend on this earth, and my sister in Christ.*

—J. Richard Coe

## PLEASE NOTE

# TABLE OF CONTENTS

# ABOUT THE AUTHORS

## TOM HALVORSON

Tom Halvorson is co-founder and chief development officer of Freestate Advisors. He has more than four decades of experience as an investment advisor, business leader, and entrepreneur. Twenty years ago, after spending the first half of his career in management consulting and business leadership, he turned his primary attention to personal investing and began evaluating the opportunities for improving the standard approach advocated by the investment advice industry. Along with his business partner at Freestate Advisors, Tom realized that the standard industry solutions had been largely unchanged since the 1960s and provided lower returns and higher risk of loss than they desired. Aware that academic research over the previous decade had uncovered numerous potential approaches to earn better returns with less risk, they began a research collaboration to develop a comprehensive strategy for improved personal investing. Their research was so successful it led them to establish Freestate Advisors and create the *SmartRisk Investment Process*™, which made their strategies available to individual and institutional investors.

Tom earned an MBA with honors from the Henry W. Bloch School of Management at the University of Missouri–Kansas City. He is a certified public accountant and CERTIFIED FINANCIAL PLANNER™ professional. Tom and his wife, Cheryl, have been married since 1974, and they have two adult daughters, Kendra and Lauren, and two grandchildren. They divide time between Kansas City and a mountain log cabin in the Black Hills National Forest of western South Dakota. Tom is an avid golfer and baseball fan, and both Tom and Cheryl are enthusiastic mountain bikers and hikers.

*Contact:*

Tom R. Halvorson
Freestate Advisors LLC
www.FreestateAdvisors.com

## J. RICHARD COE

J. Richard Coe is founder and CEO of Coe Financial Services. He is the co-author of *Retire Abundantly* and creator of the *Abundant Wealth Process*™, which helps successful business owners, professionals, and executives take a proactive approach to living their dream lifestyle. He and his team educate the public through private briefings and by exposing popular myths and mistakes that many investors are unknowingly making. They also offer other resources, including special reports, articles, and scorecards, because they understand their clients have worked hard and entrust Coe Financial Services with their money, their future, their lifestyle, and their legacy. Richard's desire is to make sure that every client can retire abundantly and fully enjoy the journey. This is a responsibility he takes very seriously.

A native of Wichita, Kansas, Richard received an MBA from the University of Chicago Booth School of Business with majors in finance and accounting. He has been a CERTIFIED FINANCIAL PLANNER™ professional since 1983. He is nationally recognized as a financial educator, author, and speaker, and has appeared on or been publicized through NBC, ABC, CBS, FOX network affiliates, *Bloomberg Business, Yahoo Finance, Investing Daily, Wall Street Select,*

*Market Watch,* and *The Wichita Eagle.* Richard and his team have been helping business owners, professionals, executives, and retirees preserve, protect, and pass on their wealth for nearly forty years. He has been married to his wife, Deb, since 1982 and they have two adult sons, David and Doug, and four grandchildren. Richard enjoys reading and traveling.

## Contact:

J. Richard Coe
Coe Financial Services
8100 E. 22nd Street N., Bldg. 1400-2
Wichita, KS 67226
www.CoeFinancialServices.com

# ACKNOWLEDGMENTS

Many people have played important roles in bringing this book to fruition. Thank you to those who read and gave constructive criticism on our early drafts of the manuscript: Tom Telthorst, Michael Thomas, Ames Stetzler, Jeannie Bush, Bob Bush, Nathan Haskins, Brett Conley, Josh Barlow, Melinda Parks, Don and Polly Peters. Thank you to my co-author and principal collaborator on this project, J. Richard Coe. Richard has great intellectual curiosity and is constantly examining his assumptions about how to get the best result for his clients. He taught me the true meaning of George Bernard Shaw's important insight: "Progress is impossible without change, and those who cannot change their mind cannot change anything." Thank you to my colleagues at Freestate Advisors for the investment research and insights that are foundational to the book, and for the time over the past year to devote myself to putting our ideas and thinking in book form. Thank you to our many clients who have been willing to listen to new ideas and think differently about the investment problem, and for what you have taught us about applying these ideas to real life. Finally, thank you to our editors and other team members at Advantage Media Group|ForbesBooks for your guidance, attention to detail, and occasional prodding to help us get this project across the finish line.

—TOM HALVORSON

It was my privilege to grow up in Wichita, Kansas experiencing love, respect, security, and support from my parents, John and Edith Coe, and my brother, Alan Coe. My parents and my brother had an appetite for learning, so a desire for learning was instilled in me quite naturally from an early age.

I have gone through life learning and have had wonderful teachers. While I could name many, I think now especially of my fifth grade teacher, Mrs. Childs, who required us to write a theme a week; my constitutional law professor, Dr. G. Theodore Mitau, who had us brief ten Supreme Court cases a week; and former Vice President Hubert H. Humphrey who taught international public affairs and who enthusiastically and passionately shared from his experience.

My Macalester College economics professors facilitated a solid foundation for me in economics and strongly encouraged me to get an MBA at the University of Chicago.

The University of Chicago had an enormous impact on the investment community's understanding of economics and financial markets. It was my great privilege to be exposed to academic giants and what was then breakthrough, cutting-edge research.

Jeremy Siegel was one of my professors at the University of Chicago before he moved to the University of Pennsylvania's Wharton School of Business. He is the author of the highly-acclaimed *Stocks for the Long Run*, but it was his March 14, 2000 article—*Big-Cap Tech Stocks Are a Sucker Bet*—in the *Wall Street Journal* that first made me start to question what I learned about Modern Portfolio Theory and efficient markets. The financial crisis of 2008-2009 made me even more doubtful regarding conventional buy and hold, "live with the bounces" thinking.

Brett Conley of Freestate Advisors patiently facilitated my deeper understanding of the stock market and played a key role in my paradigm shift. He was the one who introduced me to Benoit Mandelbrot's *The (Mis)behavior of Markets*.

Brett's partner, Tom Halvorson, had the idea for this book and honored me by asking me to help. From the beginning it has been a joy to collaborate with Tom.

My business coach, Scott Keffer, has provided wise counsel and encouragement regarding the book.

Authors Bruce McNicol, John Lynch, and Marvin Martin also provided both encouragement and insights for us.

I am very grateful for those who have served as part of the Coe Financial Services team, both past and present employees.

I also want to express appreciation for the team at Advantage Media Group|ForbesBooks who helped facilitate this book.

—J. RICHARD COE

# INTRODUCTION

*We believe life is a gift* that comes with both challenges and responsibilities. One of those challenges is money. We have a passion to help you and others more fully enjoy your hard-earned wealth. Money is a two-edged sword: mismanagement can have devastating consequences, whereas proper stewardship can yield great rewards.

This book is the product of our efforts to solve for ourselves the same problem that investors everywhere have been trying to solve. People in their forties and fifties beginning to think about the prospect of retirement, people in their sixties nearing retirement, and people already in retirement all have a common concern which you may share: What is the best way to manage your accumulated wealth to assure that you have enough for what matters? And, if you think you won't have enough, you'll want to know what you can do about it.

## OPTIONS FOR IMPROVING YOUR WEALTH OUTCOMES

The concept of "enough" is easy to understand. But what is enough? The answer depends on what matters to you, which means there are as many answers to the question as there are people. However, we know from years of working with clients that there are some common objectives.

The desire to take care of yourself financially over the balance of your life is a priority that's almost universally shared. This means having the resources to retire when desired, maintain the retirement lifestyle you've hoped for, and provide for your future health and care needs as you age. For some, this answers the question, but others have interests that extend beyond just providing for themselves. They care about helping family, friends, and charitable causes that are important to them.

If your objective is to improve your chances of having enough, or if you see the benefit of creating more for what matters beyond yourself, then the highest impact strategy available to you is to become a better investor. To understand why, let us first consider the other options for improving wealth outcomes:

**Saving more**—By the time we are contemplating retirement, the years of saving money from our salary are largely behind us, and we will soon shift to consuming what we have accumulated. Therefore, it's difficult to make much of an impact with this strategy.

**Reducing lifestyle expenses**—This is a possibility but it's not the answer most people want to hear and, in our experience, has not been a realistic strategy for most people. By retirement age, most people have settled into lifestyle spending levels that are very difficult to change.

**Working longer**—If you are age sixty-five, continuing to work until you are age seventy defers the need to withdraw from accumulated wealth for an additional five years.

While this can make a big difference, working longer is not the desired answer for many people.

**Reducing longevity**—Don't worry, we're just kidding. However, longevity is an important issue with retirement portfolios because living longer requires more resources. Therefore, how long you live will have a major impact on retirement finances. Obviously, longevity is not something we control, and even if it was, most people, given the choice, prefer a longer lifespan. Since we don't know how long we will live, and since it has a great bearing on how long our money must last, we have no choice but to assume we will live a long life. This increases the importance of becoming a better investor.

Short of hoping for a surprise inheritance, investing is the primary determinant of better wealth outcomes in retirement. For the average sixty-five-year-old couple, actuarial tables tell us there is a 45 percent chance that at least one of them will live beyond the age of ninety. That means we could be investing and withdrawing in retirement without a working income for twenty-five to thirty years. Therefore, learning to becoming a better investor in order to improve returns, reduce risk, and increase what can be withdrawn from your portfolio can be a game-changing, transformational path to having more for what matters.

These were the problems we set out to solve for ourselves nearly twenty years ago. Ultimately, we decided to write this book because what we'd learned was so important. We wanted to help individual investors understand the arguments for a better alternative to the standard portfolio management orthodoxy advocated by the investment advice industry.

## OBSTACLES YOU MAY FACE

When we ask our clients what matters most to them, the answer is rarely, if ever, "money." Having said that, clients have repeatedly told us that they want to maintain their present lifestyle, and they do not want to run out of money. You probably have similar sentiments.

What stands in your way? What obstacles might you face?

The biggest single threat to your retirement plans is probably another period like 2008–2009. If your money is in harm's way, another market meltdown could wreak havoc on your dreams for the future. The financial consequences of large losses are obvious and, as discussed in chapter 4, the odds of another major downturn in financial markets are growing. But beyond the financial impact of large losses, researchers are beginning to study the health and emotional consequences of negative wealth shocks. A recent article in the *Journal of the American Medical Association* notes that "research conducted in the wake of the Great Recession (of 2008–2009) showed significant associations between negative wealth shocks and short-term clinically relevant health changes, including increased risk of depression and anxiety, suicide, impaired cardiovascular function, and substance abuse."[1]

For many (but hopefully not you), the second largest threat to financial well-being is spending too much. Many do not know how they can adopt realistic spending habits without sabotaging their retirement future. This is not a book about how to manage or control personal spending. However, if you can improve your personal wealth

---

1    Lindsay R. Pool, Sarah A. Burgard, Belinda L. Needham, et al., "Association of a Negative Wealth Shock with All-Cause Mortality in Middle-Aged and Older Adults in the United States," *JAMA* 319, no. 13 (2018): 1341–50, doi:10.1001/jama.2018.2055.

situation by becoming a better investor, that will tend to support higher retirement spending for longer periods.

The third obstacle is even more disconcerting. About 50 percent of people will have a need for long-term care.[2] Unless those people are wealthy, eligible for government assistance through Medicaid, or have long-term care insurance, they and their spouses may experience a troubling impact on their financial future. Again, becoming a better investor to increase returns, lower risk, and improve wealth outcomes will help to address this issue.

A fourth obstacle is procrastination. Who among us is not occasionally guilty of this? While we believe the message of this book will provide benefits throughout your lifetime, it's especially timely now. *We believe most individual investors will experience poor investment returns and high risk over the next seven to ten years, severely compromising their retirement plans.* We will lay out the case for this view in chapter 4. If you read this book and the message resonates with you, you will be wise not to procrastinate. You will want to take action.

Yes, there are other obstacles to realizing your dreams, both seen and unseen. But our belief is that you can make the greatest impact on your wealth outcomes by becoming a better investor. This is the issue we will be addressing with this book.

## OUR STORY

Standard industry investment practice is based largely on Modern Portfolio Theory (MPT), which originated at the University of Chicago in the 1950s. We will delve more into this body of thinking

---

2    Melissa Favreault and Judith Dey, "Long-Term Services and Supports for Older Americans: Risks and Financing Research Brief," *ASPE*, July 1, 2015, https://aspe.hhs.gov/basic-report/long-term-services-and-supports-older-americans-risks-and-financing-research-brief.

in chapter 3. Suffice it to say that MPT is not so "modern" anymore. A significant body of academic research over the last twenty years has revealed important shortcomings in this approach, including the absence of the business cycle, belief in the constancy of investment risk, and faith in market efficiency.

Richard tells the story of how he came to question MPT after following the standard industry practice for years. Early in 2000, he read a persuasive article in the *Wall Street Journal* by his former business school professor, Jeremy Siegel, who by then was teaching at the University of Pennsylvania's Wharton School of Business. Siegel's message was that technology stocks were priced at irrationally high levels and they would inevitably fall back to earth.[3] Siegel's message was compelling, and there was nothing about his arguments that Richard could debate.

However, Richard had a problem. While pursuing an MBA at the University of Chicago in the early 1970s, he had completely embraced Modern Portfolio Theory. MPT is based on the idea that security prices are determined "efficiently," meaning they reflect all available information and are always "correct." For example, there is no such thing as stock prices being too high based on earnings or the underlying economic fundamentals. MPT assumes that stock prices are always correct at whatever level the market has determined. Therefore, according to MPT, it would be impossible for Siegel to know that technology stock prices were too high and that future prices would be much lower.

Because MPT assumes it is impossible to know anything useful about security prices or investment conditions, *this leads its adherents to the conclusion that portfolio risk management and asset allocation*

---

3    Jeremy J. Siegel, "Big-Cap Tech Stocks Are a Sucker Bet," *The Wall Street Journal*, March 14, 2000, www.wsj.com/articles/SB952997047343478041

*must be passive. In other words, portfolios should always hold the same asset classes (such as stocks and bonds) in the same proportions, no matter what.* But, if Siegel was right, then something was wrong with MPT.

At the time Siegel wrote his article, the tech-heavy NASDAQ 100 had soared to over 4,600. By September 2001, it had plummeted 75 percent to 1,150. It would be fourteen long years before the NASDAQ 100 recovered back to its early-2000 level. Later, Richard would become familiar with the work of Robert Shiller of Yale University. Shiller earned the Nobel Prize in Economics in 2013 for proving that investment conditions tell us a great deal about future security prices and risk, which is exactly what Siegel was suggesting in his 2000 article and is contrary to the assumptions of MPT.

Mindful of what happened when the technology bubble burst, Richard managed client portfolios differently during the recession and financial crisis of 2008 and 2009. When he realized the crisis was becoming ugly, he asked himself, "Why would we want our clients to have to live through this?" The standard investment orthodoxy of holding the same portfolio all the time based on MPT no longer made any sense to him. He wondered, *If we know investment conditions have become very hostile, why would we remain passive? Why wouldn't we make changes in portfolios to avoid losses and defend capital while waiting for the storm to pass?* At this point, Richard was questioning everything he'd been taught in graduate school about investment management and the approaches taken by the investment advice industry at large.

Don Peters, an eighty-five-year-old man with strong Libertarian beliefs, knew both Richard and Tom and suggested that they, along with Tom's business partner, Brett Conley, should meet. Don would be the first to admit that he is a cantankerous, salty fellow with strong views he doesn't hesitate to express. Before he founded his private investment firm, Don was chief investment officer at the largest bank in Kansas. He was also widely respected regionally and nationally for his thirty-year track record of outstanding investment returns managing portfolios at the bank and later for private investors. During his career, he had seen many investment advisors come and go spouting various ideas. Thus, he tended to be very skeptical and dismissive of other investment professionals. However, he was aware of the research Tom and Brett were doing which challenged status quo thinking, and he thought they might be on to something important. So, he recommended that Tom, Brett, and Richard get acquainted.

It was an unusual suggestion, given that they were competitors at the time. Richard was the founder and CEO of Coe Financial Services, a registered investment advisor firm, and had evaluated and dismissed many investment strategies over the years. Tom and Brett had founded a competing firm in Kansas City—Freestate Advisors— to provide active portfolio management strategies. Despite his skepticism, Richard was intrigued by their discussions involving new thinking and research on business cycles, market inefficiencies, the impact of belief systems and behavioral biases on investment management, and their concerns with industry standard investment practices and MPT.

Like Richard, Tom and Brett had immersed themselves in the standard orthodoxies of MPT and efficient market thinking while studying finance in graduate school. They worked together in management consulting for several years before going their separate ways as finance executives for public and private companies. Despite not working directly in the investment management field for the first twenty years of their careers, they had maintained an interest in investing and capital markets and stayed abreast of new developments in finance and investment research.

In 2001, Tom was doing financial consulting for a Fortune 500 company. It turned out that Brett was a finance executive at the same company. They reconnected and began discussing different approaches to investing their personal wealth. One day Brett asked, "What do you think about Modern Portfolio Theory? Do you think it's completely true as we were taught in graduate school?" Tom believed those ideas still provided the best framework for investment management and saw no reason to question them. However, Brett said he'd been doing a lot of reading over the years and was no longer so sure. He gave Tom a couple of academic papers describing new investment research, suggested he read them, and asked him to come back and revisit their discussion.

The academic papers Brett recommended opened Tom's eyes to a whole new world of important research being done at major universities to re-examine some of the underpinnings of MPT. While the standard investment solutions offered by the investment advice industry provided lower returns and higher risk than they desired, leading universities had undertaken new research that uncovered numerous potential approaches for earning better returns with less risk. As a result, Tom and Brett resolved to collaborate in the development of improved strategies for personal investing. Their personal investment success prompted them to establish Freestate Advisors to offer their strategies to other investors.

## TRANSFORMATIONAL INVESTING

While Tom, Brett, and Richard followed different career paths prior to collaborating professionally, they independently arrived at similar conclusions about the need to rethink the standard investment approach that had underpinned industry investment advice for fifty years. As they began to think seriously about how to improve their personal investing, the question they asked was not whether standard industry practice and MPT were good strategies—they are. After all, the standard approach based on MPT has been shown to be superior to what individual investors typically achieve on their own.[4] (While this is true, it is not the same as saying the standard approach is the best way to manage an investment portfolio, which we'll discuss in chapter 3.) Instead the real question was: could the industry standard of practice be improved, particularly for investors in or approaching retirement whose plans would be devastated by another downturn in the market?

Despite what they'd been taught in graduate school, they believed the answer was "yes." They knew that finance research over the previous decade had uncovered numerous potential strategies for earning better returns with less risk. It was clear that the new thinking emerging from academia had the potential to be a game-changer for retirement investing, but they also saw that the standard of practice within the investment advice industry had remained unchanged for more than fifty years and was still based on theories developed in the 1950s and 1960s.

Let's apply this approach to another field, medicine for example. Here is the question: were medical practices in the 1960s better than they were sixty years earlier in 1900? Given that by 1960 life expectancy had increased 40 percent since 1900, clearly medical practice was better in the 1960s than in 1900. However, asking whether standard medical practice in the 1960s was better is the wrong

---

4 "Dalbar's 22nd Annual Quantitative Analysis of Investor Behavior For period ended: 12/31/2015," Dalbar, 2016, https://www.qidllc.com/wp-content/uploads/2016/02/2016-Dalbar-QAIB-Report.pdf

question. The right question is: have the scientific advancements of the past fifty years made medical care better today than in the 1960s?

Obviously, the answer is "yes." Think of it this way: if you had a medical problem today (or even if you didn't), would you choose a physician who had not changed their thinking and medical practice since the 1960s? If medicine was like the investment advice industry, many of the important developments of the last fifty years would not be reflected in current medical practice.

The last major innovation for the individual investor was the development of the mutual fund. Invented in 1924, the idea began to develop broad acceptance in the 1950s and 1960s. Mutual funds are investments that pool the money of many individual investors to purchase a collection of stocks, bonds, or other securities that might be difficult for an investor to assemble on their own. The principal benefit of mutual funds is making it simple and easy to broadly diversify one's portfolio. The value of diversification is an important investment principle from MPT.

We view the investment principles and ideas in this book as another significant innovation for the individual investor and potentially game-changing for retirement investing. This is the reason for the book's title: *Transformational Investing*. A common definition of *transformational* is "a lesson or experience that inspires a shift in thinking, causing a thorough or dramatic change, especially in a way that makes it better." We believe the ideas in this book reflect those attributes:

1. they require a shift in thinking,

2. their application results in important changes in how individual investors approach portfolio management, and

3.  they require that individual investors take a different and potentially game-changing approach to the problem.

Our hope is that this book might be a catalyst for significant meaningful change in how you and other investors think about and approach the investment problem. We recognize that adoption of these concepts represents a paradigm shift for the investment advice industry. We believe that shift is overdue.

# CHAPTER 1

# THE INNOVATOR'S
# DILEMMA

*As we began the quest to improve* our individual investing, it turned out there was an important advantage we possessed, although we became aware of it only in hindsight. Our advantage was the combination of Richard's extensive experience providing client investment advice at Coe Financial Services, and the fact that Tom and Brett at Freestate Advisors came from outside the investment advice industry. This insider/outsider approach may sound like an odd combination, but it proved critical to our ability to challenge the status quo and consider new approaches to the problem. In a 2014 discussion, Brett told Richard, "If we had PhDs from the University of Chicago (the birthplace of Modern Portfolio Theory), it's likely we would never have discovered what we have. We would have been so steeped in the standard orthodoxy that it would have been very difficult to examine the problem with fresh eyes."

Clayton Christensen, a professor at Harvard University, described the problem in his book, *The Innovator's Dilemma*, published in 1997. The essence of Christensen's idea was that it's difficult for a business or industry to innovate because true innovation frequently challenges the status quo, or better defined, how the business currently makes its profits. If you are already successful with your current approach, what is the incentive to change, especially if the change threatens to undermine your existing products and services? Therefore, it's difficult for new ideas and technologies to garner development resources and executive support within an organization or industry. As a result, Christensen said, it's far easier for innovation to occur from outside the industry on the part of individuals or organizations who have nothing to lose because they have no current business to protect. In other words, since Tom and Brett came from outside the investment advice industry and sought only to improve their personal investing, they had no qualms about challenging how investment portfolios were managed if there was evidence to support a better approach.

As an example, consider the story of the former film giant Eastman Kodak. During most of the twentieth century, Kodak held a dominant position in photographic film and cameras. As late as 1976, they commanded 90 percent of film sales and 85 percent of camera sales in the United States.[5] You already know how the story ended. Digital photography eventually replaced film and the great American company Eastman Kodak is no more. The ultimate irony is that the first digital camera was invented at Kodak in 1975. However, management killed the product out of fear it would threaten their

---

5    Henry C. Lucas, *The Search for Survival: Lessons from Disruptive Technologies* (Santa Barbara: Praeger, 2012), 16.

photographic film and camera business.[6] That, in a nutshell, is the Innovator's Dilemma.

## PROBABILISTIC THINKING

*Sally has a bag filled with six green balls and two red balls. What is the probability of Sally picking a red ball from the bag?*

You might have seen a question like this on a math test at some point in your school career. Right now, though, you're probably wondering, "What does this have to do with becoming a better investor?"

A great deal, as it turns out. In fact, probabilistic thinking is one of the key reasons why Warren Buffett has become a multi-billionaire. His long-time business partner, Charlie Munger, noted in his 1994 lecture at the University of Southern California Business School, "Buffett . . . automatically thinks in terms of 'decision trees' and the elementary math of probabilities, permutations, and combinations." Munger goes on to say that everyone should understand elementary probabilities.[7]

You can rest assured that we won't be delivering a math lesson in this chapter. That won't be necessary, because probabilistic thinking is already second nature in everyday life. We will illustrate this with a few examples, and then show how this type of thinking can help readers gain a better understanding of investment strategy. We will

---

6    Nathan McAlone, "This man invented the digital camera in 1975—and his bosses at Kodak never let it see the light of day," Business Insider, August 17, 2015, http://www.businessinsider.com/this-man-invented-the-digital-camera-in-1975-and-his-bosses-at-kodak-never-let-it-see-the-light-of-day-2015-8

7    "Probabilistic Thinking and the 80/20 Rule," GuruFocus, September 10, 2007, https://www.gurufocus.com/news/13090/probabilistic-thinking-and-the-8020-rule; "Charlie Munger sobre stock picking," Think Finance, http://www.thinkfn.com/wikibolsa/Charlie_Munger_sobre_stock_picking

show why, after twenty years of research on financial markets, we believe probabilistic thinking is the key to better investing.

You are watching the evening news. The weather lady reports: "There is a 60 percent chance of rain tomorrow." As it turns out, you were planning a picnic but decide to postpone and wait for better weather. Make no mistake—you are not 100 percent certain it will rain. But you know the risk of rain is uncomfortably high, and rain would ruin your picnic, so you change your plans.

Tomorrow comes and there is no rain. Does this mean you made a mistake? Not really, because there was also a 40 percent probability of no rain. Does this mean you will stop paying attention to the weather lady? Hopefully not, if you are thinking straight. While in this instance it turned out there was no rain, your decision to cancel was still the smart move regardless of what actually happened.

Lately you have been thinking deeply about probabilities. You investigate the weather lady's methods and determine that, while nobody can accurately predict what will happen tomorrow, her information is useful in planning your picnics. You realize that if you pay attention to her, you will be more likely to make the right picnic decision than if you guess at tomorrow's weather or assume that skies will always be sunny. You reach this conclusion even though you know you won't be right all the time. The key idea is that *you will be right more often.*

Probabilistic thinking is easy to see with insurance products. You aren't shocked that your auto premiums increase when you add your teenage son to the policy, or when insurers quote higher premiums for life insurance at age fifty than at age twenty-five, even when your health is good. You understand that higher rates reflect higher risk.

Many people stop smoking tobacco or choose not to start because they believe it causes lung cancer. The Center for Disease

Control reports that smokers are fifteen to thirty times more likely to develop lung cancer than are non-smokers, but it's not 100 percent certain either way. Many lifelong smokers never develop lung cancer, and many non-smokers develop the disease in spite of their abstinence. Nonetheless, it's obvious from the data that smoking greatly increases the risk of lung cancer. Therefore, based on the increased risk (rather than a 100 percent certainty of outcome), the smart decision is to change your behavior and avoid tobacco. This is the essence of probabilistic thinking.

## APPLICATION TO INVESTING

Now we are ready to apply these ideas to investing. Most readers are probably aware that stocks are the best long-term asset class for growth, but they also have the highest periodic risk. Over the past ninety years (1928 through 2017), stocks have turned in a remarkable 10 percent compound annual return.[8] However, if you bought and held a broadly diversified 100 percent stock portfolio for that ninety-year period, you would also have endured periodic drawdowns of up to 60 percent. "Drawdown" is our preferred measure of portfolio risk and is defined as the peak-to-trough decline in value.

No matter how much you may want to earn the higher historical return from stocks, it's a rare investor who can sleep at night with that much risk. Therefore, investors are faced with a tradeoff: how much growth do they want or need versus how much risk can they tolerate?

The Standard Industry Investment Model (Standard Model), the most widely-used approach in the industry, addresses the problem by

8    Investopedia, June 2018, answer on the question, "What is the average annual return for the S&P 500?" Investopedia, https://www.investopedia.com/ask/answers/042415/what-average-annual-return-sp-500.asp

prescribing a constant percentage of stocks that depends on how the investor feels about the growth versus risk tradeoff. We coined the term "Standard Model" because the standard advice given to individual investors within the investment industry is based on some version of that model. We will explore the Standard Model in depth in chapter 3. For now, it's sufficient to say that the Standard Model prescribes a higher percentage of stocks for investors seeking more growth and who are willing to tolerate higher risk. A lower percentage of stocks will be recommended for investors willing to sacrifice growth in order to have lower risk in their portfolio. The key idea in the Standard Model is that the percentage allocation to stocks is *constant regardless of financial market conditions.*

The Standard Model is based on Modern Portfolio Theory, which assumes a constant relationship between the risk and return of stocks. If this were valid, then the best approach to managing an investment portfolio would be to maintain a constant allocation to stocks. However, we wondered whether a different approach might emerge if we added one additional piece of information that requires probabilistic thinking: financial market conditions. We suspected that the risk-return relationship of stocks is *not constant* and therefore the portfolio's exposure to stocks should *change as conditions change.*

To test our theory, we developed a methodology for objectively measuring financial market conditions. *Objective* means the measurement system was based entirely on economic and financial market data with no element of judgment or interpretation involved. This was a measure we could calculate based on objective data every single trading day for the last ninety years. The methodology was based on whether corporate profits were strong and getting better, or eroding and getting weaker. If strong and getting better, we classified those conditions as *bullish*. Strong and growing profits are an indication of a growing economy, which is generally bullish for stock prices.

On the other hand, if corporate profits were eroding and getting weaker, we classified those conditions as *bearish*. Eroding corporate profits suggest a weakening economy, which should be unfavorable for stock prices and may precede a possible slide into recession. Nearly all major losses in stocks over the past one hundred and twenty years have occurred in recessions. Therefore, the key to getting a better wealth outcome is to avoid large recession losses.

## Stock Returns and Risk by Condition
## 1928-2017

|  | Bullish | Bearish |
|---|---|---|
| Percent of Returns | 92% | 8% |
| Percent of Risk | 20% | 80% |

| Portfolio Strategy | ➤ | Bullish Conditions | More Stocks Fewer Bonds | Bearish Conditions | Fewer Stocks More Bonds |

You can see the results of the analysis for the past ninety years in the chart above. The Standard Model assumes a constant risk-return relationship. If this were true, the risk and return of stocks should be random, and bullish and bearish conditions should be similar, with each containing about 50 percent of the returns and 50 percent of the risk.

However, we found that the relationship between risk and return is far from constant. It turns out that bullish conditions contain most of the profits (92 percent of all stock returns) and a relatively small portion of the risk (only 20 percent or about one-fifth of the total), whereas bearish conditions show paltry returns and contain most of the risk with periodic losses of as much as 60 percent.

In the chart above, "percent of returns" was measured by aggregating the total returns of all periods of bullish conditions and doing the same for all periods of bearish conditions. Risk was determined by drawdown, the decline from peak to trough. Drawdowns are normal even in bullish conditions, but they were up to four times worse in bearish conditions.

*This information, coupled with a bit of probabilistic thinking, suggests a completely different approach to portfolio management than standard industry practice.* The industry's advice to individual investors is to maintain a passive, static portfolio with a constant allocation to stocks and other asset classes. However, we reached a different conclusion: portfolios should change as conditions change. This means portfolios should hold more stocks when conditions are bullish, and relatively few or no stocks when conditions are bearish. Just as it's smart for you to listen to the weather lady when planning your picnics, it's also smart to change your portfolio when conditions change. You won't be right all the time, but you should be right more often by taking advantage of this information.

Nearly twenty years after we began a concerted effort to become better investors, we can now summarize what we have learned in three principles:

1.   If you want a better result, you have to do something different. It should be obvious that following the Standard Model will yield the standard results. However, our

objective was to apply insights gleaned from leading academic research and our own research to improve returns and reduce risk in comparison to the Standard Model.

2.   Taking a different approach requires thinking differently about the problem. Sometimes a better investment approach may even be counterintuitive and contrary to our common-sense instincts in the short term. The paradox of better investing is that the solution is partly technical and partly behavioral. Granted, there are some technical improvements that must be developed and mastered. However, the primary reason it's hard for many people to become better investors is that our common-sense beliefs about investing often lead us astray. We will explore this idea in chapter 5.

3.   The highest impact strategy for changing wealth outcomes is becoming a better investor. It is not always easy, but the outcome is worth it.

You may wonder, "If these ideas are so compelling, why doesn't the industry embrace the change? After all, they have scores of smart people, huge organizations, and lots of resources. If this were a better approach, wouldn't the giants of the industry be offering it?"

The answer has much to do with the Innovator's Dilemma described previously, which goes a long way in explaining why it's extremely difficult for the investment advice industry to offer this approach on a wide-scale basis:

1.   The industry is already very successful doing what it has always done. What is the incentive to change? Think again about the Kodak example earlier in this chapter. It was impossible for Kodak management to embrace a new idea

that threatened their highly successful photographic film business.

2.  The industry has been telling customers for years that portfolio allocations should remain passive. We're hopeful you will come away from reading this book with the understanding that portfolios should change as conditions change because that's a better approach to the problem. However, it's difficult for the industry to advocate a different approach without calling into question its past advice.

3.  Most investment advisors are steeped in the application of the Standard Model. Offering a new approach would represent a massive retraining effort for the industry.

4.  Actively managing portfolios based on investment conditions is more labor intensive for the industry and investment advisors than keeping portfolios the same under all conditions. If you are already successful attracting clients with the current approach, there is no incentive to embrace a more labor-intensive approach.

5.  The industry's present business model is built on the idea of passive, static investment portfolios. The operational, information system, and business process logistics of implementing a more flexible approach to portfolio management would be a massive and hugely expensive undertaking for the industry.

6.  The final reason the industry is unlikely to change may be the most important. Individual investors are not clamoring for a better alternative. If customers demanded a better

approach, new solutions would emerge, but so long as their customers are content to follow the Standard Model, there is no incentive for the industry to do anything different.

*We believe individual investors are not demanding a better alternative because they have been educated to believe there is no better alternative.* Our clients often say they believed the Standard Model was the best and only approach because that is what they had always been told. In fact, many have gone on to say they always thought there should be a better approach and that it seems logical to change portfolios when conditions change, but no one was offering any alternatives. We hope this book will help to change that situation by educating individual investors about a better alternative to standard portfolio management.

> *We believe individual investors are not demanding a better alternative because they have been educated to believe there is no better alternative.*

CHAPTER 2

# CHANGE YOUR THINKING, CHANGE YOUR OUTCOME

*Tom met George when he was randomly assigned* to be his playing partner in a local golf tournament. The sixty-three-year-old George has his own business as a contractor for home renovation and is a self-described "refugee from the corporate world." By this he means that he used to be a sales and marketing executive for companies supplying equipment to engineering firms. George has always enjoyed doing projects around the house, and over a period of several years he completely renovated their one hundred-year-old home. About ten years ago, he decided to quit the corporate world and start his own business doing what he loved—working on home renovations.

George's wife Stephanie has her own successful career as a business litigation attorney with a mid-sized law firm. Stephanie is also sixty-three. They have been married for more than forty years and have three adult children, all of whom live in other cities. They have no planned date to retire but expect to begin winding down their work lives over the next couple of years.

While playing golf, George learned that Tom was in the investment business. George told Tom that he and Stephanie had worked with a financial advisor for several years and proudly proclaimed that, unlike most people he knows, they did not lose any money in the financial crisis of 2008 and 2009. He said their advisor had moved them to safe investments before the big downturn. Instead of large losses in the period, they had a small single-digit gain. Tom congratulated George on that outcome and confirmed that most people had experienced large losses and great emotional angst during that period.

Their attention turned back to golf, but later George raised the topic of investments again. "Stephanie is concerned that our advisor is being too conservative," he said. "Since 2009, our portfolio has been 50 percent stocks and 50 percent bonds. It seems to me that our returns have been decent but not great, but we also know that stock market returns have been very strong for the last eight years. It's really starting to bother Stephanie that we are not fully participating in the bull market for stocks. She is concerned that we are falling behind and missing out on additional stock gains in our portfolio. Now that we are starting to think about retiring in the next couple of years, she thinks we are not maximizing our investment opportunities. She thinks we should be investing more aggressively. What do you think?"

## THE MILLION-DOLLAR INVESTMENT LESSON

George and Stephanie have a critical ingredient of a better approach right in front of them, and they don't even realize it. There is an important lesson that can be learned from their situation and the questions they are asking. We call it the Million-Dollar Investment Lesson, and we've written this book to illustrate its principles. The lesson involves learning to think differently about the investment problem, even when it may seem counterintuitive.

As the title of this chapter suggests, we believe you can dramatically change your long-term investment outcome, but only if you are willing to change your thinking and approach. To illustrate, let's look at a hypothetical couple in their early sixties. They are looking ahead to retirement and will likely have a twenty-five-to-thirty-year investment horizon over the balance of their lives. For each $1 million they have accumulated in their current portfolio, would our hypothetical couple be willing to think differently about the investment problem if the payoff was an extra million dollars or more earned over the balance of their investing lives? We think that's a realistic expectation if investors are willing to faithfully apply the lessons of this book.

## WHICH INVESTMENT IS BETTER?

Let's start the discussion with a question. The chart on the next page shows two stock investments and their performance over a recent eight-year period. Both portfolios are broadly diversified and composed of the stocks of large, high-quality US companies. Which investment would you prefer for your portfolio?

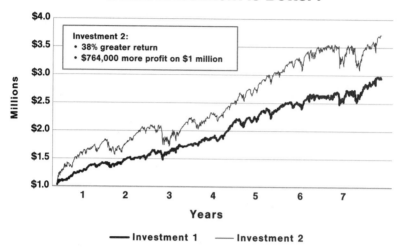

## Which Investment is Better?

Investment 2:
- 38% greater return
- $764,000 more profit on $1 million

Based on eight years of historical performance—which most investors would consider a sufficiently long period to judge an investment strategy—everyone picks stock investment two because it has done much better over that period. The performance difference is large and steady across a relatively long period of time. Investment two has outperformed investment one by 38 percent over this period and generated $764,000 more profit on an initial investment of $1 million.

When we use this example in discussions about investment strategy, no one has ever chosen stock investment one, and nobody asks any questions or requests any additional information before making that decision. The choice seems obvious.

The truth is there is not enough information for you to make an informed decision about which investment is better. If we look at the chart below, however, we see how these two investments have performed over a longer period—sixteen years.

## Now, Which Investment is Better?

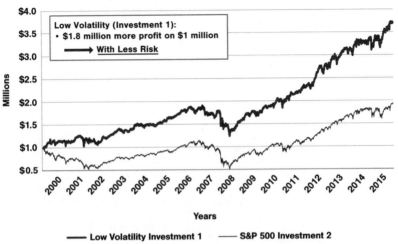

Investment two is the S&P 500, and investment one is a low-volatility cohort of the S&P 500, which consists of S&P 500 stocks with lower price volatility. Lower volatility simply means they tend to vary less in their daily price movements than the stock market average.

The result shown above is surprising to many individual investors, especially when they learn that the superior investment (low-volatility stocks) lagged the S&P 500 some 78 percent of the time and yet delivered nearly three times the cumulative profit with less risk. During the period above, low-volatility stocks had a worst drawdown of 35 percent, while the S&P 500 had a worst drawdown of 55 percent. This translates to about one-third less risk. *Drawdown* is our preferred measure of portfolio risk and refers to the percentage peak-to-trough decline of an investment. The less drawdown in a portfolio, the better.

---

9   For this illustration, we used the twenty-five lowest volatility S&P 500 stocks each month based on the trailing average twenty-day volatility drawn from the largest 60 percent of the S&P 500 by market capitalization.

Let's repeat that information. Low-volatility S&P 500 stocks trailed the broad S&P 500 index some 78 percent of the time and yet delivered nearly three times the cumulative profit with one-third less risk.

How can that be? It defies common sense. It's contrary to our understanding of how the investment world works. However, academic research shows that this result is not surprising. Since its discovery forty years ago, there have been many academic studies showing that low-volatility stocks outperform the stock market with less risk over the long run. A few examples include Jangannathan and Ma (2003),[10] Clarke De Silve and Thorley (2006),[11] and Baker, Bradley and Wurgler (2011).[12] Additionally, low-volatility stock performance versus the S&P 500 turns out to be quite predictable.

*Studies have shown that low-volatility stocks consistently lag when the market is rising but lose less when the market declines.*

Studies have shown that low-volatility stocks consistently lag when the market is rising but lose less when the market declines.

## IS THIS THE MILLION-DOLLAR INVESTMENT LESSON?

You might be wondering if investing in low-volatility S&P 500 stocks is the Million-Dollar Investment Lesson. After all, in the example

---

10  R. Jagannathan, and T. Ma, "Risk reduction in large portfolios: Why imposing the wrong constraints helps," *The Journal of Finance* 58, no. 4 (2003): 1651–1684, https://doi.org/10.3386/w8922.

11  Roger Clarke, Harindra de Silva, and Steven Thorley, "Minimum-variance portfolios in the US equity market," *Journal of Portfolio Management* 33, no. 1 (2006): 10–24, https://doi.org/10.3905/jpm.2006.661366.

12  Malcom Baker, Brendan Bradley, and Jeffrey Wurgler, "Benchmarks as Limits to Arbitrage: Understanding the Low-Volatility Anomaly," *Financial Analyst Journal* 67, no. 1 (2011): 40–54, https://doi.org/10.2469/faj.v67.n1.4.

above, $1 million invested in low-volatility stocks generated $1.8 million more profit over a sixteen-year period than did the same $1 million invested in the broad S&P 500 index. Clearly, low-volatility stocks seem to be a far better stock investment than the mutual funds and exchange-traded funds (ETFs) most individual investors hold in their portfolios. If readers did nothing more than substitute a low-volatility S&P 500 ETF for any broadly diversified stock mutual fund or ETF in their portfolio, they would get more than their money's worth from this book.

However, that is not the Million-Dollar Investment Lesson. As we will illustrate in subsequent chapters, portfolios should change when conditions change, and an investor's objective should be to hold the best investment assets for the current conditions, whatever they may be. With this illustration, we have demonstrated that low-volatility stocks are a better "buy-and-hold" stock asset for investors who are following a passive strategy in managing their portfolio. But if you accept the premise of this book and are committed to changing your portfolio as conditions change, there are always better investment assets for your portfolio than low-volatility stocks for both favorable and unfavorable investment conditions. The reason is that low volatility stocks lag in favorable conditions and often have large drawdowns in unfavorable conditions (although less than the broad stock market).

Instead, we are simply using the low-volatility stock effect to illustrate a point. *The real power of the Million-Dollar Investment Lesson comes from understanding what causes the low-volatility effect.* Why do low-volatility stocks consistently outperform the broad stock index over long periods? Once we understand why this is true, we can begin to understand the Million-Dollar Investment Lesson and are on the road to changing how we think about portfolio management.

# INSIGHTS FROM THE LOW-VOLATILITY EFFECT

As we said earlier, low-volatility stocks represent companies whose daily stock prices are less volatile than the overall stock market. *Lower volatility* simply means they vary less in their daily price movements than the stock market average.

Low-volatility stock prices vary less because they represent companies whose earnings are less sensitive to conditions in the economy. *Less sensitive* means they hold up better when times are bad, but they don't grow as fast when times are good. They are the "steady Eddies" of the S&P 500. The eight-year period of under-performance for low-volatility stocks shown above was a period of economic growth. Low-volatility stocks always lag the market in those conditions. However, low-volatility stocks also lose less than the market average when conditions are unfavorable.

For example, Procter & Gamble, a company that produces a variety of consumer products such as toilet paper, hand soap, and toothpaste, is less sensitive to what happens in the economy than, say, Starbucks, which relies on more discretionary expenditures. It's easy to see how a company like Starbucks, which sells expensive coffee drinks, is more sensitive to economic conditions than a company that sells toilet paper and toothpaste. When economic conditions worsen, consumers are far more likely to cut back on discretionary spending than on essentials.

Likewise, when the economy grows, low-volatility stocks don't grow as fast as the market average. In the example above, low-volatility stocks lagged the S&P 500 when the economy was growing, which turned out to be 78 percent of the time over a sixteen-year period.

The first insight from the low-volatility effect is basic portfolio math. Simply stated, *minimizing losses is far more powerful for wealth outcomes than maximizing gains.* In other words, protecting capital is paramount. An investor who loses 50 percent must generate a 100 percent return just to get back to even. That's a difficult hurdle to clear.

As noted earlier, low-volatility stocks had a worst drawdown (peak-to-trough decline) of 35 percent versus 55 percent for the S&P 500. Because low-volatility stocks do a better job of controlling losses in the downturns, they start from a higher base when the market recovers. That higher base results in a performance difference that's hard to overcome. Therefore, even though low-volatility stocks grow slower most of the time, it takes a long time for the faster-growing S&P 500 stocks to catch up after a downturn, if ever.

The second thing we can learn from the low-volatility effect is the *importance of the business cycle in determining investment risk and return.* We will have a great deal more to say on this topic in later chapters. For now, it's sufficient to note that the business cycle refers to the natural growth and contraction of the economy. Stock returns and the risk of holding stocks follow the business cycle. Stock risk is lower when the economy is growing. The reason: profits grow when the economy grows, and stock prices rise when profits grow. This is because stocks represent an ownership interest in the profits of a company.

However, stock risk is high when the economy contracts, as it does periodically. When the economy contracts, corporate profits drop significantly, and stock prices react violently to the decline in profits. These periods of contraction in the economy are called *recessions.* Nearly all major stock market losses have occurred during recessions.

The following chart divides the performance of low-volatility stocks versus the S&P 500 between periods of expansion when the economy is growing and periods of recession when the economy contracts.

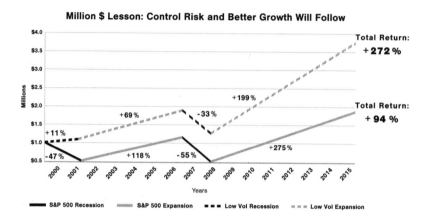

**Million $ Lesson: Control Risk and Better Growth Will Follow**

You can see that the S&P 500 grows faster than low-volatility stocks during periods of expansion. However, low-volatility stocks are better at controlling risk in recessions, and that matters far more than getting all the gains. As a result, low-volatility stocks come out miles ahead.

We know there is always a business cycle with both large gains and large losses. We also know that minimizing losses affects portfolio growth far more than maximizing gains. Therefore, paying close attention to the business cycle and avoiding recession losses—even at the expense of missing some gains—is a recipe for a better outcome. That's a powerful idea, often missing from the minds of financial advisors and individual investors.

## THE FAILURE OF COMMON SENSE

This raises the question: if the idea is so powerful and makes such a difference, why is it often missing from our thinking? The answer is what Duncan J. Watts—an author and a principal researcher at

Microsoft Research and a former professor at Columbia University—calls the "failure of common sense." In 2011 he published a book entitled *Everything Is Obvious: *Once You Know the Answer*. This is not a book about investing, but the ideas it expresses have important implications for becoming a better investor.

Drawing on the latest scientific research, Watts shows in his book how common-sense reasoning conspires in duping us into thinking we understand complex systems and relationships better than we do. In a chapter entitled "The Myth of Common Sense," Watts says, "Common sense is great for everyday problem solving, but 'problems' to do with government planning, policy, business, and marketing are not like everyday problems . . . Common sense is simply not designed to solve these sorts of complex problems, *but its limitations are rarely apparent to us.*"[13]

We can see the failure of common sense at work in the low-volatility stock example. Everyone picks the wrong investment when they see eight recent years of lagging performance. We see individual investors make the same errors when comparing investment outcomes over much shorter periods of time. The predictable thought process says: "My investment lagged over the last two years. It's not working. I need to make a change."

The usual reason given for choosing the investment with better recent performance is that it is obvious. However, the correct choice is anything but obvious. People consistently choose the wrong investment because of our natural human tendency to oversimplify complex situations. In the field of behavioral economics, this is known as a *heuristic bias*, meaning a short-cut decision rule that leads us to the wrong conclusion. We will have a great deal more to say about the

---

13   Duncan J. Watts, *Everything is Obvious: *Once You Know the Answer*, (New York: The Crown Publishing Group, 2011), emphasis added.

field of behavioral economics, particularly on biases and their importance to the portfolio management problem, in chapter 5.

The consistent mistake investors make when considering the low-volatility stock decision discussed above is due to *recency bias*. This has been well documented by behavioral economics researchers. Recency bias states that we are all prone to extrapolate the recent past into the future. Our thinking is greatly influenced by what has happened recently. We weigh recent events more heavily in our thinking, even though there is no rational basis for that assumption. In other words, without really thinking it through, we make a quick decision based on an underlying belief that the future will look like the recent past. Therefore, if an investment has done better for the last eight years, we think it will do better in the future.

In the low-volatility stock example, when investors oversimplify the problem and choose the wrong investment, two elements are missing from their thinking, and *it's the missing elements that make all the difference*. The first thing missing is an understanding of the power of minimizing losses. Controlling losses affects portfolio growth far more than maximizing gains. The second thing missing is the business cycle, which drives nearly all investment risk and return. For a long-term investor, the only returns that matter are those earned over the complete business cycle. It does an investor no good to earn high returns during good economic times only to lose it all in the next recession. This is why we preach that avoiding large losses always yields better long-term results than maximizing gains.

# CHANGE YOUR THINKING,
# CHANGE YOUR OUTCOME

Let's go back to George and Stephanie's situation. You recall that George bragged about missing the downturn of 2008 and 2009, but more recently he and Stephanie have grown disenchanted with their subpar returns. They feel their current advisor is being too conservative with a 50 percent stock and a 50 percent bond allocation. With retirement on the horizon and a strong stock market, they feel they are falling behind and missing out on additional stock gains in their portfolio. Stephanie thinks they are not maximizing their investment opportunities and should be investing more aggressively.

George wanted Tom's opinion, so they arranged to meet at Tom's office to talk further. Tom asked George to send him some past data on their portfolio performance beforehand so he could do some analysis in preparation for the meeting.

About a month later, George and Stephanie went to his office. In that time, George had done some analysis on his own. George began the meeting by presenting the results of his analysis. He noted that since the market bottom in March 2009, their portfolio had lagged the stock market by 180 percent.

"We have been behind for eight years, and I think it's time to make a change. We need a more aggressive investment strategy to take advantage of stock market gains," he told Tom. Stephanie agreed.

Tom said he would be happy to help them, but after reviewing their portfolio and past history, he said his conclusion might surprise them. He noted that their current advisor's investment strategy had helped them avoid the losses of 2008 and 2009 and even generated a small profit of 5 percent in that period. He said, "If you'd held an all-stock portfolio invested in the S&P 500 during the same period, you would have experienced a 55 percent drawdown from the peak in late 2007 to the market bottom in March 2009.

"It's true that the stock market has done much better than your portfolio since the stock market bottom, and that outperformance has been going on for a number of years," Tom said. "And we agree that when the economy is growing and investment conditions are bullish, as has been the case since 2009, a 50 percent stock allocation is too low for most people. You should hold more stocks when conditions are bullish and few or no stocks when conditions are bearish.

"But, that is far from the whole story," he added. "We think your investment strategy has been more successful than you think. By far the most common mistake individual investors make is to oversimplify complex situations and make investment decisions based on what has happened recently. Because they are not seeing the whole picture, individual investors are often led astray by what they regard as basic common-sense thinking. The best answer to your problem may seem obvious, but in fact, the best answer is not obvious at all. Let me explain.

"Based on your questions, you are focusing on stock performance because that asset class has done well lately. However, you would probably be surprised to learn that the investment strategy you want to abandon has outperformed an all-stock portfolio by 100 percent over the complete business cycle. That means you have earned double the profits of an all-stock strategy. And, you haven't had to endure the emotional distress of experiencing large losses in your portfolio. So, I'd have to say you have done exceptionally well with your current strategy, far better than most people and far better than you realize."

Tom went on. "There are two things missing from how you are thinking about your situation. The first thing missing is the idea that avoiding large losses matters far more than getting all the gains. This idea is very counterintuitive. Most individual investors believe the opposite. They think getting all the gains is more important than avoiding large losses, and they get extremely caught up in chasing recent investment returns.

"The second thing missing is the business cycle. The recent past may seem like the relevant period to judge an investment strategy, but that is not true. Instead, the entire business cycle is the relevant period for a long-term investor. George, your analysis showing lagging results since March 2009 reflects only the part of the business cycle when the economy was growing. Your analysis ignored the recession. In fact, stocks have done worse than your current strategy over the whole cycle because they sustained big losses in the recession.

"It is also important to note that we are in the late innings of the current business cycle. When the next recession comes, stocks will once again sustain large losses. We don't know exactly when that will occur and neither does anyone else. But the evidence suggests it will happen sooner rather than later. So, you are thinking about becoming more aggressive just in time for the next recession. That is probably not what you had in mind.

"We are big believers in the idea of getting as much of the gains from favorable conditions as possible, and there is a good chance there will be additional gains from stocks over the next couple of years. So, we agree that you could increase your stock allocation beyond 50 percent of the portfolio. But there is a caveat. You can't focus exclusively on the prospect of stock market gains. You must remain vigilant about avoiding the upcoming recession losses. Avoiding losses matters far more than getting all the gains. Your past portfolio performance attests to that principle. If you abandon a strategy that helped you avoid losses in the last recession to chase the last couple years of good stock returns, in our view you will be making a big mistake and your retirement plans will suffer."

How is it possible they have earned twice the return of stocks even though they've lagged far behind the past eight years? Because George and Stephanie didn't lose in 2008, their portfolio started its growth in the subsequent expansion phase from a much higher base. So, even though the all-stock portfolio has roared ahead recently compared to their more conservative 50 percent stock/50 percent bond portfolio, they have still come out 100 percent ahead. Plus, we know that business cycles don't last forever, and there will be another recession sooner rather than later, with more losses for stocks similar to those of the last two recessions. Because of the impact of the business cycle, it is doubtful that the all-stock portfolio will ever catch up to George and Stephanie's results.

After reviewing these figures, the pair admitted that the situation looked quite a bit different than they had imagined. They realized, despite what they thought was just basic common sense, that avoiding losses is the most important factor in determining portfolio outcomes and they needed to think of their portfolio performance in the context of the entire business cycle. They realized they were getting caught up in the excitement of recent stock market performance and that making an investment decision based on what has happened recently didn't make a lot of sense since it ignored the business cycle and therefore had little or no bearing on what would happen in the future.

What shocked them most was finding that their current investment strategy which they'd regarded as "too conservative" had resulted in them being miles ahead despite the roaring stock market. George and Stephanie came away from the meeting with a new appreciation for what they had accomplished and an openness to changing their thinking about how best to manage their wealth over the balance of their lives.

## THE MILLION DOLLAR INVESTMENT LESSON: TWO CRITICAL INSIGHTS

Over the course of twenty years of investment research to find a better way to invest our personal wealth, two critical insights stand out which together are the essence of the Million Dollar Investment Lesson we referred to earlier. The first is that *long-term investment results are determined primarily by losses, not gains.* The better investment is the one that does a better job of controlling losses even if it lags during favorable conditions. In other words, the more successful investor is almost always the one who avoids large losses, even if to do so means they miss some of the gains. It's the basic math of portfolio growth.

The second critical insight is that *gains and losses in financial markets are driven by the business cycle.* If you know that minimizing losses is the key to getting a better outcome, it is essential to pay attention to the business cycle and investment conditions. It also means there is no such thing as an investment asset for your portfolio that is the best in all conditions. Portfolio assets must change as conditions change. These are the ideas we'll be exploring in the following chapters.

# CHAPTER 3

# SOMETHING IS MISSING

*If you are like most individual investors* and have sought invest-ment advice or researched on your own to design a portfolio strategy, you are probably familiar with the following process:

**Step 1**: Determine your risk tolerance. This might be based on a discussion of your attitudes about investing, investment experience, age, retirement status, and the need and desire for portfolio growth. You may have even completed a standard questionnaire asking how you feel about certain investment outcomes, such as periodic losses. Whatever the approach, you end up being assigned to a risk category ranging from "low" risk tolerance to "high" risk tolerance.

**Step 2**: Based on your assigned risk category, a standard portfolio model is prescribed. That model will include a percentage alloca-tion to different types of investments, such as stocks and bonds. If you have a low tolerance for risk and don't need much growth, lots of bonds and few stocks will be prescribed. On the other hand, if you have a high tolerance for risk and/or you need higher portfolio growth to meet your financial goals, more stocks and fewer bonds will be prescribed.

**Step 3**: Thereafter, unless there is a major change in your situation, you are advised to always maintain the prescribed percentage allocation among the different types of investments. There may be a recommendation that your portfolio be reviewed annually and, if the percentage allocation has drifted from the prescribed model portfolio, it should be "rebalanced" back to the original recommended percentages. However, the essence of the advice is that you should maintain your model allocation at all times. In other words, no matter what investment conditions you may encounter, your portfolio should always remain the same and hold the same percentage of stocks and bonds in all conditions.

If this sounds familiar, you are not alone. The process outlined above is, in one form or another, the standard approach for advising, designing, and managing investment portfolios within the investment advice industry. Investment advisors have been recommending and following this approach since the 1960s. Depending on the investment advisory firm or investment company, it may have more steps, describe things a bit differently, or vary from one situation to another in minor ways. But, at its core, the process is always the same and is largely as described in the three steps above.

Because this is the standard approach in the investment industry, we'll refer to it as the Standard Industry Investment Model, or Standard Model for short. Because most investment advice is based on some version of the Standard Model, any discussion of how best to invest must begin here. Many individual investors have been told or are under the impression that the Standard Model is the best and only way to design and manage a portfolio. So, in this chapter, we'll be exploring the Standard Model, its underpinnings in financial theory, and both its merits and shortcomings. This discussion will lay important groundwork for later chapters in which we explore the possibility of thinking differently about how to approach the portfolio management problem.

## GARY AND MARTHA'S PORTFOLIO DILEMMA

Gary and Martha have been saving and investing for many years, and over the last decade their focus shifted from accumulation to withdrawing from their portfolio for retirement. When they were sixty years old in 2008, their portfolio had just recovered from the 2001–2002 recession and market downturn, and they were hoping their portfolio would continue to grow as they approached age seventy. Unfortunately, things turned out differently than they hoped.

In the spring of 2008, they moved to a new town and put their old home on the market. The stock market was declining, and they were very anxious. Thankfully, despite declining real estate prices, they were able to sell their home and they came out okay. However, they were not so fortunate with their investment portfolio.

During the recession and financial crisis of 2008 to 2009, their $1.3 million investment portfolio dropped almost 40 percent. Although they didn't know it at the time, even if they weren't withdrawing from their portfolio to support retirement, it would take six years of strong stock market returns to recover their losses. In other words, it would take them six years just to get back to where they started.

However, because they were retired and withdrawing from the portfolio, they never really recovered from the losses of the recession. From their perspective, they were doing what they'd always been told based on the Standard Model advocated by the investment advice industry. Gary felt like they were adrift, and Martha was having a hard time sleeping at night.

"With all the smart people working in this area, there should be a better way to do this," Martha said. She felt they had trusted the investment industry, and it was failing them at just the time they most needed help.

## MODERN PORTFOLIO THEORY AND THE STANDARD MODEL

The Standard Model is based on the set of ideas contained in Modern Portfolio Theory (MPT). MPT originated in 1952 when Harry Markowitz, then a PhD student at The University of Chicago, proposed that investors could construct portfolios to maximize their expected return based on a given level of market risk. MPT emphasizes that greater risk is an inherent part of getting a greater investment reward.[14] Nearly forty years later, Markowitz won the 1990 Nobel Prize in Economics for this work.

We can see MPT at work in the Standard Model with the following illustration:

---

14  "Modern Portfolio Theory (MTP)," Investopedia, accessed 2018, http://www.investopedia.com/walkthrough/fund-guide/introduction/1/modern-portfolio-theory-mpt.aspx#ixzz4tKbcN07X.

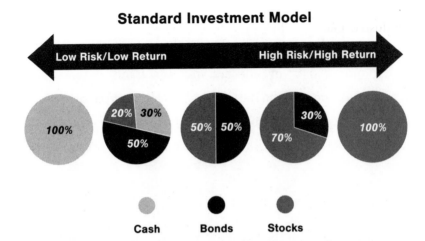

**Standard Investment Model**

Low Risk/Low Return          High Risk/High Return

100% | 20% 30% 50% | 50% 50% | 30% 70% | 100%

Cash    Bonds    Stocks

This is a common illustration of the process of designing an investment portfolio. Portfolio models range from low risk to high risk, and, consistent with MPT, greater risk is assumed to be associated with higher investment returns over time. Investors determine where they fit on the risk and return spectrum which, in turn, suggests a model portfolio with a mix of investment assets yielding the desired risk profile.

For the sake of simplicity, this illustration shows only three asset classes: cash, bonds, and stocks. Cash is considered the lowest risk and lowest return, while stocks are considered the highest risk and highest return over time. As the desired return and associated risk profile increases, the portfolio composition shifts from safe and very low return to risky and higher return. Stocks represent the growth assets of a portfolio because historically they have, on average, produced higher returns with higher risk. Bonds and cash are considered the safety assets of the portfolio because they have produced lower returns with lower risk.

The Standard Model takes a passive approach to managing portfolio risk by setting an unchanging allocation among investment assets depending on the investor's tolerance for risk. More stocks and fewer bonds are recommended for investors seeking growth and who are able to tolerate higher risk. Fewer stocks and more bonds and cash are recommended for investors desiring less risk and who are willing to sacrifice portfolio growth. The key idea is that the percentage allocation among cash, bonds, and stocks is fixed. It's always the same regardless of investment conditions. This is the Standard Model in a nutshell.

## BENEFITS OF THE STANDARD MODEL

There are important benefits to following the Standard Model. First, it provides discipline. It is well established in financial research that individual investors, left to their own devices and emotions in making portfolio decisions, fare very poorly. Below is one artist's view of investment decision-making by some individual investors.

**Happy Trading...**

*Slope of Hope, accessed 2018, https://slopeofhope.com/socialtrade/item/1868.*

The reason for this behavior is that people are highly emotional when it comes to their money. When they see their portfolio dropping, they panic. Once burned, they tend to sit out most of the next round of favorable returns because they're scared after the last bad experience. Often, they get back in on the tail-end of an expansion period—just before the contraction that comes at the end of a business cycle—and they ride the market down once again. Then, having been burned once again, they sell at the bottom and miss the gains from a rebounding market.

We see evidence of this behavior today. Individual investors still have vivid memories of the turmoil and large losses of the recession and financial crisis of 2008 to 2009. As we write this in 2018, we have now seen eight years of strong stock returns. However, according to Gallup, stock ownership among Americans plummeted from 65 percent in 2007 to 52 percent in 2016, tied for the lowest level of stock ownership since the organization began tracking it in 1998.[15]

As we said, the ideas expressed above have been borne out with years of solid research. Since 1994, Dalbar Inc., an independent investment research firm, has published an annual report entitled *Quantitative Analysis of Investor Behavior.* The report seeks to measure the effects of individual investor decisions to buy, sell, and switch into and out of various investment vehicles.

The results have shown consistently over the years that the average investor earns much less than asset class performance would suggest. For example, through 2015, the twenty-year annualized return of the S&P 500 was 8.19 percent, while the average individual equity investor earned only 4.67 percent over the same period.

---

15    Justin McCarthy, "Just Over Half of Americans Own Stocks, Matching Record Low," Gallup, April 20, 2016, https://news.gallup.com/poll/190883/half-ameri-cans-own-stocks-matching-record-low.aspx.

In other words, individual stock investors have underperformed the market over the past twenty years by 43 percent. Dalbar concludes that the average investor's performance is weak because he or she gets in late, is reactive to short-term market conditions, and doesn't stay invested long enough to participate in market expansion.[16] Thus, by prescribing a fixed and unchanging portfolio allocation, the Standard Model provides an important element of discipline that individual investors often lack.

A second important idea that comes into the Standard Model from MPT is the benefit of diversification in reducing risk. MPT classifies risk as either *systematic* or *specific*. Systematic risk can be thought of as *market risk*. The stock market rises and falls, and all stocks are similarly affected because they are part of the broad market.

Specific risk simply means the risk of an individual security. For example, think about a $1 million portfolio invested entirely in a single stock, such as Enron. Enron was a high-flyer for many years. However, the company ultimately failed due to management fraud, costing employees and investors tens of billions of dollars.[17] That's an example of the risk of an individual security.

In MPT, specific risk or individual security risk can be reduced through diversification. In the example above, instead of just one stock, MPT would suggest holding a broadly diversified portfolio of perhaps one hundred stocks. If your portfolio held one hundred stocks in equal amounts, only one of which was Enron, the fact that Enron collapsed and disappeared would be disappointing, but

16   "Dalbar's 22nd Annual Quantitative Analysis of Investor Behavior For period ended: 12/31/2015," Dalbar, 2016, https://www.qidllc.com/wp-content/uploads/2016/02/2016-Dalbar-QAIB-Report.pdf

17   Kurt Eichenwald, "Enron's Collapse; Audacious Climb to Success Ended in Dizzying Plunge," *The New York Times*, January 13, 2002, https://www.nytimes.com/2002/01/13/us/enron-s-collapse-audacious-climb-to-success-ended-in-a-dizzying-plunge.html

because it only represented 1 percent of the portfolio it would not be a disaster. That's an example of using diversification to reduce individual security risk.

Nevertheless, even if you held a broadly diversified portfolio of one hundred stocks, they would all tend to rise and fall with the overall market. If the stock market declined 50 percent (as often happens during recessions), then chances are that the total value of your portfolio of one hundred stocks would also decline about 50 percent. In other words, while diversification reduces individual security risk, no matter how diversified your stock portfolio, there is no escaping systematic or market risk for an asset class such as stocks or bonds. Even if you held a thousand stocks, your stock portfolio would rise and fall the same amount more or less as the overall market. The Standard Model embraces this idea by prescribing broad diversification within asset classes in constructing the portfolio. This is an important and beneficial idea from MPT.

A third important idea that comes into the Standard Model from MPT is the importance of asset classes over security selection in determining risk and return outcomes. Stated in simpler terms, as long as you are broadly diversified within an asset class—such as stocks—risk and return is affected far more by *whether you hold stocks* than by *which stocks you hold.* A study published in 2000 by Ibbotson and Kaplan found that 90 percent to 100 percent of the risk and return performance of a portfolio is determined by the percentage allocation among the major asset classes of stocks and bonds.[18] This means that nearly all portfolio risk and return is determined by the allocation of the portfolio among asset classes, and very little

---

18    Roger G. Ibbotson, and Paul D. Kaplan (2000), "Does Asset Allocation Policy Explain 40, 90, or 100 Percent of Performance?" *Financial Analysts Journal* 66, no. 3 (May/June 2010): 45–59.

is determined by the individual securities you (or your mutual fund manager) select within each asset class.

This idea is at the heart of the Standard Model. Stocks are the growth engine of a portfolio by virtue of their long-term return track record. However, they also have higher periodic risk. The overall stock market has periodically experienced peak-to-trough declines of as much as 50 percent to 60 percent. Therefore, if you seek greater portfolio growth and are willing to tolerate greater periodic risk, the Standard Model recommends allocating a greater percentage of the portfolio to stocks. As long as your stock portfolio is broadly diversified, it matters far more whether you hold stocks than which stocks you hold. This is a direct application of an important idea from MPT in the Standard Model.

In summary, we wholeheartedly agree with these important attributes of the Standard Model. It provides discipline, requires broad diversification to reduce risk, and is built on research that shows that asset allocation determines nearly all of the risk and return outcome of a portfolio. As shown by the Dalbar studies, following the Standard Model provides major benefits versus the results individual investors typically achieve when investing on their own.

## SOMETHING IS MISSING

As we studied the problem in order to improve our own investing practices, it became clear that something important was missing from the Standard Model. For example, the most fundamental assumption of MPT and the Standard Model is the relationship between risk and return. In other words, if you are willing to assume more risk, you will be rewarded with more return.

However, our research showed this was not true more than half the time. We found that nearly 60 percent of the time over the past ninety years, a higher risk portfolio has not yielded a higher return.[19] In other words, 60 percent of the time the most fundamental of assumptions underlying the Standard Model and MPT is not true!

We continued our research and ultimately uncovered the missing ingredient: an understanding of how the business cycle affects portfolio risk. Let's go back over the Standard Model once more to examine this important idea.

Investment portfolios are constructed primarily from two asset classes: stocks and bonds. A portfolio may contain different varieties of the two asset classes, for example, growth, value, large cap, small cap, international, emerging markets, corporate, government, etc. An investor may even sprinkle in a small bit of real estate, commodities, or precious metals, but nearly all investment portfolios boil down primarily to stocks and bonds.

As noted above, stocks are considered the growth engine of an investor's portfolio, and with good reason. Over the long term, the inflation-adjusted return from stocks is three times the return from bonds.

If this was all we needed to know, an investor would always hold a 100 percent stock portfolio. However, it's not that simple. An investor who is always 100 percent invested in stocks must be prepared to tolerate periodic declines of more than 50 percent. That happened twice between 2000 and 2010. It is rare to find investors who can tolerate that much risk. Moreover, while stocks have always

---

19    For this analysis, we compared the after-inflation returns of a higher risk portfolio (80 percent stocks/20 percent bonds) to a lower risk portfolio (20 percent stocks/80 percent bonds) between 1929 and 2017. We found that the higher risk portfolio did not produce a higher return during 1929–1948, 1969–1982, and 2000–2017 representing nearly 60 percent of the time during that period.

recovered, the recovery often takes five to six years and the declines can be devastating if they occur when the investor is withdrawing from their portfolio in retirement.

This is the basic dilemma of investing. Investors want growth, and stocks are the best source of growth for an investment portfolio. However, the risk of an all-stock portfolio is more than most investors can bear. What's an investor to do? *The answer to this question is where we part company with the Standard Model.*

The Standard Model takes a passive approach to managing portfolio risk by setting an unchanging allocation among investment assets depending on the investor's tolerance for risk. More stocks and fewer bonds will be recommended for investors seeking growth and who are able to tolerate higher risk. Fewer stocks and more bonds will be recommended for investors desiring less risk and who are willing to sacrifice portfolio growth. The key idea is that the percentage allocation among cash, bonds, and stocks is fixed. It's always the same, regardless of investment conditions.

As we said, this is where we part company with the Standard Model. The reason is the Standard Model assumes that stock risk is constant, always high and completely random. It assumes that large losses appear out of nowhere and could happen at any moment. However, our research shows this is not true. Instead, the risk of holding stocks varies significantly depending on economic conditions and the business cycle. Despite this, *the business cycle is nowhere to be found in the Standard Model.*

The *business cycle* refers to the natural growth and contraction of the economy. Stock returns and the risk of holding stocks follow the business cycle. Stock risk is lower when the economy is growing. The reason: profits grow when the economy grows, and stock prices rise when profits increase. Profit growth is what makes stock prices go up.

This makes sense because stocks represent an ownership interest in the profits of a company.

However, stock risk is high when the economy periodically contracts. When the economy contracts, corporate profits drop significantly, and stock prices plummet. These periods of contraction in the economy are called recessions. Nearly all major stock market losses have occurred in recessions.

The following chart shows the impact of the business cycle on stock prices. Solid periods represent growth in the economy, while dashed periods are recessions when the economy is shrinking.

**S&P 500 Adjusted for Inflation**

*Data from Robert Shiller, Yale University.*

The chart shows that the risk of holding stocks depends primarily on the business cycle. Risk is lower when the economy is growing and higher when the economy enters recession. Note that "lower risk" does not mean "no risk." While stock prices have increased during periods of economic growth, they do not go up in a straight line. There is still a fair amount of zigging and zagging with some periodic corrections on the way up. However, the key point is that risk is not constant nor random, and it does not originate from some unknown source. Instead, it's clear that the risk of holding stocks varies considerably, and this is driven by economic conditions and the business cycle.

This is the key insight that "changes everything" in comparison to the Standard Model. Because the Standard Model assumes stock risk is constant, always high, and completely random, portfolios are typically underinvested in stocks during times of economic growth and overinvested in stocks during recessions. Because portfolios are underinvested when the economy is growing, portfolio growth is sacrificed. And because they are overinvested during recessions, large losses are sustained.

This insight is important for two reasons: First, it should prompt us to reexamine our assumptions about how best to manage investment portfolios. We'll examine this in later chapters. Second, if financial market risk and return are not random but are determined by the business cycle, then an ability to understand where we are in the business cycle should help us understand the investment environment that lies ahead. We will discuss this more in the next chapter.

# CHAPTER 4

# THE ROCKY ROAD AHEAD

*Before venturing on a long road trip,* a rational person would say, "The roads are dry and skies are sunny, so I am going to drive fast because conditions are favorable for driving and therefore it's not risky. However, when the road gets icy or a winter storm hits, it's risky to drive fast so I am going to slow down and be careful." Over the course of a long road trip, we don't expect driving conditions to be the same all the time. Sometimes they will be favorable for driving fast, and sometimes they change for the worse. When this happens, the smart thing to do is slow down or even pull over for the night and wait for the storm to pass.

In this chapter, we will present the case that the business cycle determines road conditions for investors, and that all business cycles include dry roads and sunny skies as well as icy roads and stormy weather. In addition, we will show that because, at the time of writing, we are in the "late innings" of the current business cycle, icy roads and stormy weather are likely sooner rather than later. As a result, investors following the standard investment model will experience poor returns and high risk over the next seven to ten years, and their portfolios will fail to do the job they need them to do. To avoid this outcome, investors will need to change their thinking and change their approach.

## THE BUSINESS CYCLE

As mentioned in chapter 2, favorable conditions for economic growth are the normal state of affairs. For example, since 1947, the US economy has grown at an annual compound rate of 3.22 percent. When the economy is growing, we call these periods *expansions*. However, the economy doesn't grow at the same speed all the time, and it doesn't grow 100 percent of the time. Periodically the economy shrinks a bit, and we call these periods *recessions*. The entire cycle of economic expansion followed by recession is referred to as the *business cycle*.[20] When it comes to investment management, these cycles are the key to becoming a better investor and avoiding the fate of poor future returns and high risk.

Investment conditions are favorable when the economy is expanding and corporate profits are growing. In our road trip metaphor, these periods represent dry roads and sunny skies. We can drive fast, meaning we can hold lots of stocks in our portfolio. The risk is relatively low because conditions are very favorable for that asset class. But eventually we're going to have icy roads and a winter storm, and it's going to be very dangerous to drive fast. These are periods of recession when the economy shrinks, corporate profits

---

20   For more on the history of business cycles, see "US Business Cycle Expansions and Contractions," *The National Bureau of Economic Research*. Available at www. nber.org/cycles/cyclesmain.html.

plunge, and stock prices take a beating. In these conditions, it makes sense to slow down or even pull off the road. In other words, we should reduce or avoid holding stocks in our portfolio and favor safety assets, such as US government bonds. Just as you pay attention to road conditions when you are driving, you need to pay attention to the business cycle and investment conditions when investing.

*Just as you pay attention to road conditions when you are driving, you need to pay attention to the business cycle and investment conditions when investing.*

## STOCKS AND THE BUSINESS CYCLE

We have long periods of expansion when the economy grows. This happens for a number of reasons, including productivity increases, favorable interest rates, and tax policy changes. Productivity improves as a result of the interplay of technology and education and worker training. When the interest rate environment is favorable, companies can borrow at reasonable rates to invest in plant and equipment and new technologies and development. Tax policy that allows accelerated depreciation, for example, encourages businesses to invest in plant and equipment.

Stock returns and the risk of holding stocks follow the business cycle. As the economy grows, company profits also grow, and aggregate stock prices increase. Profit growth is what makes stock prices go up. This makes sense because stocks represent an ownership interest in the profits of a company. For example, ownership of a lemonade stand that makes $200 is more valuable than the same lemonade stand making $100. The process of growing profits over time increases stock prices. If profits never grew, then stock prices would remain constant, and there wouldn't be any growth benefit to owning stocks. In times of economic expansion, therefore, it's profitable to be invested in stocks. In fact, over the last ninety years the stock market has averaged a 14 percent annual return *when the economy is expanding.*

However, from time to time, the economy shrinks a little, perhaps by 2 percent or 3 percent. That decline in economic activity has an enormous impact on corporate profits. When the economy contracts, corporate profits drop significantly, and stock prices react violently to the decline in profits. In a garden-variety recession, corporate profits may plunge by 50 percent. In the recession and financial crisis of 2008, corporate profits declined 100 percent.

As this book is going to press, we are experiencing a long period of economic expansion. Corporate profits are strong and stocks are at or near record highs, with a total return of more than 300 percent since the lows during the last recession a decade ago. In addition, bonds have produced one of their best thirty-six-year runs in history. Therefore, with those numbers in our rear-view mirror, it's reasonable to ask: what lies ahead in financial markets? More of the same or something different? We don't mean what will happen tomorrow, next month, or even next year. Rather, what should you expect from financial markets over the next seven to ten years, and what is the best course of action for you as an investor?

## HOW THE MACHINE WORKS

Let's begin with a recent quote from Ray Dalio, founder and chief investment officer of Bridgewater Associates, the world's largest private investment fund, managing $150 billion in assets. Dalio is a legend in the investment industry and, when he speaks, people listen. In a *Business Insider* interview on April 17, 2017, Dalio had this advice for individual investors: "You can expect that your future investments returns are going to be very low. *You can know that.*" [21]

What is interesting about the Dalio quote is that he views poor future returns as an inevitable outcome. We agree.

Dalio is famous for speaking about investing as something that requires an understanding of "how the machine works." If you know how it works, you are dealing with certainty. In this case, he is saying that future returns for standard "buy-and-hold" investment strategies will be low. How can he be so certain? Let's unpack his statement to answer these questions.

First, let's return to our road trip metaphor. Imagine we are taking a long road trip. Our trip will last several days, and we'll encounter a variety of road conditions. Most of the time, skies will be sunny, and the roads will be dry, but we also know there will be hazardous conditions along the way. We are anxious to get to our destination in good time, but we also want to travel safely and don't want to crash into the ditch.

We use this metaphor to help clients understand the business cycle: the process of economic expansion and recession. Nearly all investment risk and return is driven by the business cycle. The business cycle and its impact on returns and investment risk is shown in the following chart of the S&P 500.

---

21   Ray Dalio, interview with *Business Insider*, April 17, 2017, www.businessinsider. com/blodget-on-why-dalio-says-investment-returns-will-be-low-2017-4

*Data from Robert Shiller, Yale University*

In our metaphor, periods of dry roads and sunny skies represent economic expansion. Those are the solid lines shown in the chart. During these conditions, returns are good and investment risk is low. On the other hand, recessions are winter storms when losses are large, and risk is high. Those are the dashed lines shown in the chart.

This is the first step in understanding Dalio's assertion. He knows there is always a business cycle that drives investment return and risk, and there are always recessions that cause large losses. That's how the machine works.

## WE ARE IN THE LATE INNINGS

Next, we need to know how long business cycles usually last and where we are in the current cycle. We can begin to answer those questions with data from the National Bureau of Economic Research (NBER), the organization designated by the government to keep the official scorecard for the US business cycle. The following table summarizes some data from that organization:[22]

---

### US Economic Expansion History:
- Longest ever: 120 months (in the 1990s)
- Current expansion: 111 months (as of Sept. 2018)
- Third-longest: 106 months (in the 1960s)
- Historical average: 60 months

Source: National Bureau of Economic Research

---

As we write in late-2018, the current economic expansion is nine years old and is now the second-longest expansion since NBER's data began in 1854. The post-war average for expansions in the US is five years. The longest expansion on record is ten years.

Another way to understand where we are in the business cycle is to analyze what is known as the *yield curve*. Two senior economists of the Federal Reserve Bank of New York, Arturo Estrella and Frederic S. Mishkin, concluded that "the yield curve . . . is a valuable forecasting tool. It's simple to use and significantly outperforms other financial and macroeconomic indicators in predicting recessions two to six quarters ahead."[23]

A yield curve is a line that plots current market interest rates of bonds having equal credit quality but differing maturity dates. The yield curve is normally upward sloping with the longer maturities, facing more future unknowns about economic growth and inflation, commanding higher interest rates than their shorter-maturity counterparts. The yield curve is commonly analyzed by subtracting the

---

22  National Bureau of Economic Research, "US Business Cycle Expansions and Contractions," *NBER.com*, www.nber.org/cycles/cyclesmain.html.

23  Arturo Estrella, and Frederic S. Mishkin, "The Yield Curve as a Predictor of U.S. Recessions," *Current Issues in Economics and Finance* 2, no. 7 (June 1996): 1–6.

yield on short-term maturities from the yield on long-term maturities. The higher the result, the steeper the yield curve.

As the business cycle matures, the yield curve tends to flatten. This means the yield on longer and shorter maturities moves closer together, and the difference between the long end and short end of the curve gets smaller. This is in response to a combination of slowing growth expectations hitting the long end of the curve and tighter monetary policy hitting the short end. Both of these factors are capable of derailing an economy at the tail end of its expansion.

We can see the results of this analysis and the relationship of the yield curve to the occurrence of past recessions in the following chart.[24]

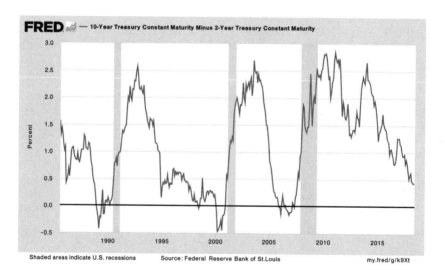

This chart shows the steepness of the yield curve by subtracting the yield on two-year treasury bonds from the yield on ten-year treasury bonds. The flatter the curve, the closer the result is to the 0.0 line. You can see that the yield curve becomes flatter as the business

---

24   "10-Year Treasury Constant Maturity Minus 2-Year Treasury Constant Maturity," *The Federal Reserve Bank of St. Louis*, April 11, 2018, www.myf.red/g/jh8W.

cycle progresses. The shaded portions are recessions. Currently, the yield curve is the flattest it has been in ten years. You can also see that ten-year minus two-year treasury bond yields often turn negative prior to recessions. This is a condition known as an *inverted yield curve*, when short-term rates are actually higher than long-term rates. In March 2018 Bauer and Mertens of the Federal Reserve Bank of San Francisco noted that every US recession in the past sixty years was preceded by an inverted yield curve. They concluded that the yield curve "is by far the most reliable predictor of recessions."[25]

Nobody knows exactly when the next recession will occur. If the current expansion continues for another year (beyond this writing), it will set a new record as the longest since 1854. It's certainly possible that could happen. But expansions don't last forever, and it's hard to see this one lasting beyond another couple of years. So, it's clear from the NBER data and from the yield curve data that we are in the late innings of the current expansion. This is the second part of understanding Dalio's comment. He knows the next recession will occur sooner rather than later.

## STOCK VALUATIONS ARE HIGH

There are different ways of determining the valuation level of the stock market. Using a method popularized by Yale University Professor Robert Shiller, winner of the Nobel Prize in Economic Sciences in 2013, the third observation is that stock prices are currently very high in relation to company earnings. Shiller's approach, which uses normalized earnings over the prior ten years, shows stock prices are

25  Michael D. Bauer, and Thomas M. Mertens, "Economic Forecasts with the Yield Curve," FRBSF Economic Letter, Economic Research, March 5, 2018, https://www.frbsf.org/economic-research/publications/economic-letter/2018/march/economic-forecasts-with-yield-curve/.

nearly double the long-term average.[26] They have only been this high twice before: in 1929 before the crash that led to the Great Depression, and at the peak of the technology stock bubble in 1999 before the major recession losses of 2000 to 2002. The following chart shows the relationship between stock prices and normalized earnings.[27]

## Normalized S&P 500 Price-To-Earnings Ratio (Shiller P/E)

Data by Robert Shiller, Yale University.

However, before anyone leaps to the conclusion that it's time to *immediately* sell all their stocks, please read on. In our research, we have found this information does not predict imminent losses in the stock market, because high stock prices can always go higher, and they can go higher for a while. Earlier, we suggested it is possible that the current economic expansion could last another couple of years. We see nothing in our indicators to suggest that we are on the cusp of a recession at present. Therefore, if this expansion lasts two

---

26    The Shiller approach refers to the Shiller PE ratio for the S&P 500, which shows the price earnings ratio based on average inflation-adjusted earnings from the previous ten years.

27    According to data compiled by Robert Shiller of Yale University and Freestate Advisors, stock prices have only been this high twice before.

more years, it's likely that stock prices will go even higher and those near-term returns could be very attractive.

However, the key point is this: knowing stock prices are high is useful in understanding future long-term returns. Prices can always go higher for a while, but they do not stay high forever. Eventually the business cycle turns, and the recession comes. *High stock prices always mean poor future returns.* This relationship is illustrated in the chart below, which gets to the heart of what Dalio is saying. It shows historical ten-year average future returns from various beginning stock valuations using the Shiller PE Ratio.

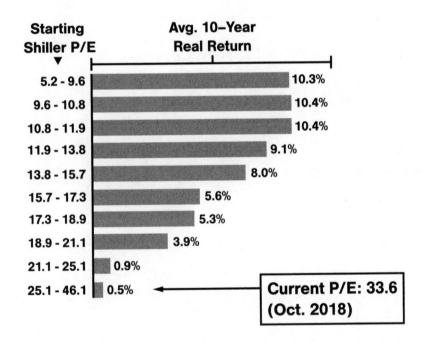

*Data by Clifford Asness, AQR Capital Management.*

Again, what we see in this chart is exactly what we should expect. When valuations start low, ten-year future returns are very good. This is because the stock market rises from low valuations to higher valuations over time. However, when valuations start high, ten-year future returns are poor. This is because high stock valuations always come back to earth. Stock valuations are currently very high. Historically, ten-year future returns from such a high valuation have been very low. This is how the machine works.

In summary, while high current stock valuations might go higher over the next year or two, they are certain to go lower over the longer term. This will create stock market losses and result in poor long-term returns. This is because of the business cycle and the impact of recessions.

## BACK TO THE BUSINESS CYCLE

To see how this all plays out, let's return to the previous business cycle chart, but with some additional information. In the chart below, we see that despite long periods of strong gains for stocks, there was a nearly sixteen-year period in the recent past when stock investors earned nothing after inflation from price appreciation. The reason was the impact of two recessions, and recessions are what destroy portfolio returns.

Remember that one of the underlying premises of the Standard Model and MPT is that if you take higher risk with stocks, then you will earn higher returns. That's true on average over really long periods of time, such as the past ninety years. However, there have been long periods within that ninety-year period when the assumption was simply not true because of the business cycle and the impact of recessions. Sixteen years is a long time to earn no real price return when you are withdrawing from your retirement portfolio.

## S&P 500 Adjusted for Inflation

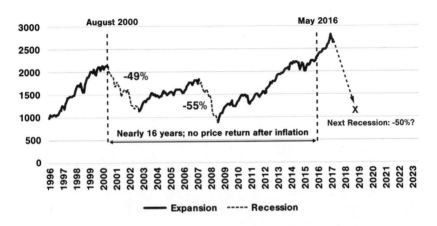

You can also see that the strong stock gains of the current economic expansion will be largely erased in the next recession. This is why we always say that the only returns that matter for long-term investors are those earned over the complete business cycle, i.e. the whole cycle of economic expansion and recession. Nine or more years of great stock returns won't matter if they are lost in the next recession.

In our road trip metaphor, periods of dry roads and sunny skies represent economic expansion. During these conditions, returns are good and investment risk is low. Recessions are winter storms where losses are large, and risk is high. After twenty years of research on how to be a better investor, we concluded that the portfolio must change when investment conditions change. We hold more stocks when driving conditions are favorable, and few or no stocks when the danger hits. The key to getting a better long-term investment

> *Nine or more years of great stock returns won't matter if they are lost in the next recession.*

outcome is to protect your money when financial market conditions are hazardous.

However, if you follow the Standard Model advocated by the investment advice industry, you will drive the same speed whether road conditions are good or bad. In other words, your portfolio will always hold the same percentage of stocks, no matter what.

## WHAT ABOUT BONDS?

Bonds are the other aspect of the portfolio that help us to understand Dalio's view of future returns. Unfortunately, the prospects for bonds are no better than those for stocks.

Interest rates have been declining for thirty-six years. By some measures, they are near the lowest level in five thousand years. To make the same point another way, recent bond prices have been higher than they have been for a long time.[28]

There is a bit of inverse-math you will have to tolerate in order to understand the outlook for bonds. Falling interest rates increase bond returns. The reason is that bond values rise when interest rates decline. This means investors receive both interest payments and increased bond values. As you can see in the following chart, inflation-adjusted bond returns over the past thirty-six years have been very good because of declining interest rates.[29]

28   James Freeman, "The 5,000-Year Government Debt Bubble," *The Wall Street Journal*, August 31, 2016, https://www.wsj.com/articles/ the-5-000-year-government-debt-bubble-1472685194.

29   Freestate Advisors analysis using data from Robert Shiller, Yale University.

## Rising and Falling Interest Rates

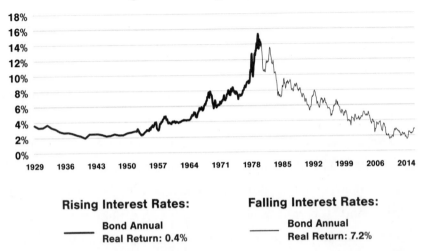

**Rising Interest Rates:**

———— Bond Annual
Real Return: 0.4%

**Falling Interest Rates:**

———— Bond Annual
Real Return: 7.2%

However, the long period of declining interest rates with exceptional bond returns is at an end. Interest rates have gone about as low as they can go. With rates this low, there are only two possible scenarios ahead, and neither will be kind to bond investors.

The first possible scenario would be for interest rates to stay at their current low level for a very long time. This is the scenario that has played out in Japan over the past thirty years. If this happens, then there will be no change in the current situation—bond investors will continue to earn little or no return after inflation.

The second possible scenario is one of rising interest rates. With current rates low, individual investors might be inclined to welcome the prospect of earning greater interest on their bonds. However, the important thing to understand about bonds is that rising interest rates destroy bond returns.

For example, assume Jack lends John $100 at the current market interest rate of 4 percent. This is what a bond represents—a loan from one party to another. When you buy a bond, you're locked in to the interest rate specified in the bond, in this case 4 percent per year. If John later decided he no longer wanted to hold the bond, he would need to sell it to someone else. If the market interest rate when he sells the bond is still 4 percent, someone will be willing to pay him $100 for the bond. However, if the market interest rate has increased from 4 percent to 8 percent, a prospective purchaser could otherwise invest his money in other bonds and get an 8 percent return. Why would he pay $100 for a 4 percent return bond when he could pay $100 and get an 8 percent return on bonds offered in the open market? Therefore, rational purchasers will offer less than $100 for the bond. They will demand a discount on the original face value of the bond sufficient for the 4 percent interest to yield the equivalent of an 8 percent return. This is the reason bond values always move in the opposite direction of market interest rates.

The nomenclature in the investment industry for this idea is that bond prices move inversely to interest rates. Falling interest rates increase the value of bonds. The reverse is also true. Rising rates reduce the value of bonds. Therefore, if interest rates rise in the future, as many expect, then bond investors will receive higher interest payments, but the higher interest will be offset by the declining value of the bonds. As you can see in the previous chart, during the last period of rising interest rates (approximately thirty-two years from 1950 to 1982), the average annual real total return (after inflation) for bonds was only 0.4 percent per year.

Former Federal Reserve Chairman Alan Greenspan told CNBC recently that the bond market is on the cusp of a collapse due to this prolonged period of low interest rates.[30] Keeping interest rates low

---

30    Alan Greenspan, interview with *Squawk Box,* CNBC, August 4, 2017, www.cnbc. com/2017/08/04 /greenspan-bond-bubble-about-to-break-because-of-abnor- mally-low-interest-rates.html

has been part of US monetary policy since 1987. After the 2008 financial crisis, the Fed took its benchmark rate to near zero and held it there for seven years. As we write, the Fed has begun raising short-term interest rates, and while more increases are expected in the future, bond yields remain low.

"I have no time frame on the forecast," Greenspan said in the interview. "I have a chart which goes back to the 1800s and I can tell you that this particular period sticks out. But you have no way of knowing in advance when it will actually trigger." Greenspan's view is that interest rates have no place to go but up.

The central banks of the world (led by the US Federal Reserve) have engaged in massive monetary stimulus since the financial crisis of 2008 to 2009. Many believe this monetary experiment (called *quantitative easing*) is not likely to end well. Just as there can be bubbles in technology stocks and housing prices, so there can also be bubbles in bonds. We have no way of knowing whether there is a bubble in bonds that will burst and lead to higher rates, or if rates will remain low for a very long time. However, for investors looking ahead, it doesn't matter which scenario you pick. There are only two possible outcomes, and both spell trouble for bond investors.

## PUTTING IT ALL TOGETHER

Now that you understand why Ray Dalio forecast poor long-term investment returns for both stocks and bonds in the future—two points become clear. First, you can't drive your portfolio by looking in the rear-view mirror. The next ten years will look nothing like the recent past in terms of standard portfolio returns. Second, the standard industry practice of driving your portfolio at the same speed all the time no matter the conditions will produce the poor investment outcome Ray Dalio anticipates.

There are certain knowable elements in investing. We know that there is always a business cycle, and the business cycle is the primary factor determining risk and return in the stock market. We know that stock valuations are very high by historical standards, and we also know that future returns are always poor from high valuations. We know we are in the late innings of the current business cycle. While nobody knows when the next recession will occur, given the late stages of the current expansion, it will likely occur sooner rather than later.

In the bond market, we understand the inverse relationship between interest rates and bond prices, and we know that interest rates are at historic lows. From here, we know that interest rates will either stay low or rise. Both scenarios are a recipe for very low long-term bond returns.

With this understanding of the investment environment that lies ahead, a different approach is needed. Portfolio holdings must change in response to the conditions we encounter. We should drive fast when the roads are dry and risk is low, but need to slow down or even get off the highway when the winter storm hits. This all seems very logical and straightforward. However, as we'll discuss in the next chapter, it is easier to be logical about driving than about our investment portfolios.

# CHAPTER 5

# THINKING ABOUT THINKING

*Two psychologists*—one a Holocaust child and adviser to the Israel Defense Forces, and the other a former paratrooper in the Israeli army—met and began a research collaboration in the late 1960s at Hebrew University in Jerusalem. Their work changed our understanding of how we think and the decisions we make with important consequences for investors.

The two are Daniel Kahneman and Amos Tversky, respectively. Over the years, they co-wrote a series of papers that revolutionized our understanding of financial and economic thinking. In 2002, Kahneman was awarded the Nobel Prize in Economic Sciences for his role in their groundbreaking work. Tversky's death in 1996 prevented him from sharing the award.

Their work uncovered the concept of behavioral biases, which are strange anomalies of human nature that cause our reasoning to go wrong. Dismissed as a backwater of academic research for years, these ideas evolved into the mainstream field known as behavioral economics. Its insights are considered among the most important developments in finance and economics of the last twenty-five years.

The central insight of behavioral economics could not be more important for investors. Simply stated, it's now a broadly accepted fact that human reason, left to its own devices, relies on mental shortcuts and biases in decision-making that routinely lead investors to irrational decisions. Behavioral biases have nothing to do with intelligence. No matter how smart someone may be, mental shortcuts and biases are hard-wired in everyone and always present. In other words, none of us are as rational and clear-thinking as we'd like to believe we are.

Therefore, if our objective is to become better investors and find a solution to the problems we've been discussing, it is important to understand how our natural biases and patterns of thinking often lead us astray. If we understand our natural biases, and if none of us are immune to their effect (no matter how smart we may be), awareness of their impact on our investing decisions is a critical part of creating a better outcome. These are the topics we'll be exploring in this chapter.

## RICHARD THALER'S STORY

If Kahneman and Tversky are the beginning of the story of behavioral economics, Richard Thaler of the University of Chicago is an example of how far the field has come. Thaler was recognized with the Nobel Prize in Economic Sciences in 2017.

Thaler's professional story began when he was a newly conferred PhD and lowly assistant professor of economics at the University of Rochester. While trying to find his way as an academic and a researcher, he spent time toying with a set of ideas. He was trained in classic economic theory, which is based on the idea that human beings are completely rational when making financial decisions. However, Thaler had noticed some inconsistencies in human behavior. He had a big whiteboard in his office and kept a list of incongruities as he encountered them. At the time he didn't know what to do with the list, or even if the incongruities were important enough to warrant further study.

In chapter 3 of his book *Misbehaving: The Making of Behavioral Economics,* Thaler offers some examples from his whiteboard list to illustrate behavior that's inconsistent with classic economic theory:[31]

- Jeffrey and I somehow get two free tickets to a professional basketball game in Buffalo, normally an hour and a half drive from where we live in Rochester. The day of the game there was a big snowstorm. We decide not to go, but Jeffrey remarks that had we bought the tickets (rather than received them as a gift), we would have braved the blizzard and attempted to drive to the game.

- Lee's wife gives him an expensive cashmere sweater for Christmas. He had seen the sweater in the store and decided it was too big of an indulgence to feel good about buying it. He is nevertheless delighted with the gift. Lee and his wife pool all their financial assets; neither has any separate source of money.

- Linnea is shopping for a clock radio. She finds a model she likes at what her research has suggested is a good price, $45. As she is about to buy it, the clerk at the store mentions that the same radio is on sale for $35 at a new branch of the store, ten minutes away, that's holding a grand

31   Richard H. Thaler, *Misbehaving: The Making of Behavioral Economics,* (New York: W. W. Norton & Company, 2015).

opening sale. Does she drive to the other store to make the purchase? On a separate shopping trip, Linnea is shopping for a television set and finds one at the good price of $495. Again, the clerk informs her that the same model is on sale at another store ten minutes away for $485. Same question ... but likely a different answer.

Thaler goes on to explain: "Each example illustrates a behavior that's inconsistent with economic theory. Jeffrey is ignoring the economists' dictum to 'ignore sunk costs,'" meaning money that has already been spent. The price we paid for the tickets should not affect our choice about whether to go to the game. Lee feels better about spending family resources on an expensive sweater if his wife made the decision, although the sweater was no cheaper. If Linnea spends ten minutes to save $10 on a small purchase but not a large one, she is not valuing time consistently."[32]

Shortly after Thaler started his informal project documenting inconsistencies in human reasoning, he ran into a colleague at a conference who was doing research on similar anomalies and had written a paper on a concept he called the *hindsight bias*. It turned out that this colleague had studied at Hebrew University under Daniel Kahneman and Amos Tversky. After much discussion of their mutual interests, the colleague suggested that Thaler might benefit from reading some of their early papers.

When he returned to Rochester, Thaler headed to the library and found a paper published by Kahneman and Tversky in 1974, titled "Judgment Under Uncertainty: Heuristics and Biases."[33] Thaler

---

32  Thaler, *Misbehaving*: 21.

33  Amos Tversky, and Daniel Kahneman, "Judgment under Uncertainty: Heuristics and Biases," *Science, New Series* 185, no. 4157 (September 27, 1974): 1124, 1131. http://psiexp.ss.uci.edu/research/teaching/Tversky_Kahneman_1974.pdf.

writes, "as I read ["Judgment Under Uncertainty"], my heart started pounding the way it might during the final minutes of a close game. The paper took me thirty minutes to read from start to finish, but my life had changed forever. The thesis of the paper was simple and elegant. Humans have limited time and brainpower. As a result, they use simple rules of thumb—heuristics—to help them make judgements."[34]

Thaler was smitten with these ideas and felt validated that somebody else was also thinking about them. He went on to read everything he could find by Kahneman and Tversky and decided to devote himself to what was then the embryonic field of behavioral economics.

Professional academics were incredibly resistant to the early groundbreaking work of Kahneman and Tversky, and it took years for these concepts to be accepted. The Israeli duo endured no small amount of professional abuse before the tide began to turn, but they and others like Thaler persisted and sparked a revolution in economic thinking.

Professionals working in the field of behavioral economics now widely accept the idea that people are wired with natural biases or mental shortcuts that cause them to make mistakes and act against their own best interest. It turns out that being a better investor is not just a technical exercise, it also requires an understanding of how we think and what motivates our behavior.

*People are wired with natural biases or mental shortcuts that cause them to make mistakes and act against their own best interest.*

34    Thaler, *Misbehaving*, 21–22.

## COMMON SENSE AND THE
## MONTE HALL PROBLEM

In chapter 2 we discussed the work of Duncan J. Watts on the limitations of common sense. What we routinely refer to as *common sense* is
just another term for the *rules of thumb* or *heuristics* that Kahneman
and Tversky identified in their work. Drawing on the latest scientific
research, Watts showed how common sense reasoning conspires in
duping us into thinking we understand complex systems and relationships better than we do.

As another measure of how far the field of behavioral economics
has come since its early days, even mainstream, non-economist,
general interest publications such as the *New Yorker* have tackled
the topic. In June 2012, Jonah Lehrer noted, "While philoso-
phers, economists, and social scientists had assumed for centuries
that human beings are rational agents, . . . Kahneman, the late
Amos Tversky, and others . . . demonstrated that we're not nearly
as rational as we like to believe." Lehrer goes on to say that "when
people face an uncertain situation, they don't carefully evaluate the
information or look up relevant statistics. Instead, their decisions
are based on mental shortcuts which often lead them to make
foolish decisions. These shortcuts aren't a faster way of doing the
math; they're a way of skipping the math altogether."[35]

A well-known illustration of the limitations of common
sense is the "Monte Hall problem." It's a reasoning problem using
the famous game show as the illustration vehicle. Most people
reading this book will remember the televised game show *Let's
Make a Deal*, starring Monte Hall. Assume you are playing the

---

35  Jonah Lehrer, "Why Smart People Are Stupid," *The New Yorker*, June 12, 2012.
    Available at www.newyorker.com/tech/frontal-cortex/why-smart-people-
    are-stupid.

game. You are shown three doors and are told that behind one of the doors is a new car, and behind each of the other two doors is a booby prize—a goat.

Monte Hall then asks you to pick a door. You have no prior knowledge of which door contains the car. Therefore, you have an equal chance of winning, no matter which door you pick. Your odds of success are one-third regardless of which door you pick. In this case, let's assume you pick door one.

## 3 Doors and 1 Car

Once you've made your pick, Monte Hall opens one of the other doors. He reveals there is a goat behind door two. He then asks if you would like to change your choice of door. You are free to stay with your original selection of door one, but you can change your selection to door three if you desire. Monte says, "Those are your choices—what do you want to do?"

The real question in this problem is: *does it matter whether you change your selection?* In presenting this example to clients many times, we have found that the universal answer is: "No, it doesn't matter whether you change your selection." The consensus view is that you have an equal chance of winning the car whether you remain with door one, your original selection, or change it to door three. Everyone calculates the odds at 50/50 either way. Therefore, it seems that the correct answer is obvious.

It also turns out that the "obvious" answer is wrong. This is a perfect example of how common sense reasoning leads us astray. If we think a bit more deeply about the problem, we can see why we are all prone to make this mental mistake.

The correct answer is: *we should always change our selection.* If you always change your selection, you will double your odds of winning the car. Here is why.

At the beginning of the game, there is a one-third chance the car is behind any of the individual doors. This means there is a two-thirds chance the car is behind *either* of the two doors you don't pick, one or the other. So, in this case, there's a one-third chance the car is behind door one, and a two-thirds chance that it is behind *either* door two or door three. So far, so good.

Then, Monte Hall opened door two to reveal a goat. When we play the game with clients and get to this point, they quickly leap to the conclusion that nothing has changed. Therefore, it doesn't matter whether we stay with door one or change to door three; it is 50/50 either way.

However, they miss an insight of critical importance: the knowledge that a goat resides behind door two is *new information that changes the odds of the game*. While the correct answer seemed obvious, nobody realized that the odds had changed because of new information. Talk about leaping to conclusions!

If there was a two-thirds chance of *either* door two or door three containing the car behind it, and we now know that door two contains a goat, that means there is a two-thirds chance the car is behind door three and your original pick, door one, still only has a one-third chance of winning. Therefore, if you change your answer, you will double your chances of winning the car.

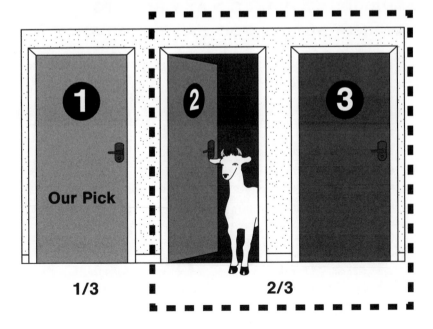

This problem was originally posed and solved in a letter by Steve Selvin to the *American Statistician* in 1975. It became famous as a question from a reader's letter quoted in Marilyn vos Savant's "Ask Marilyn" column in *Parade Magazine* in 1990.[36]

> *"Many readers of vos Savant's column refused to believe switching is beneficial, despite her explanation. After the problem appeared in Parade, approximately ten thousand readers, including nearly one thousand with PhDs, wrote to the magazine, most of them claiming vos Savant was wrong. Paul Erdos, one of the most prolific mathematicians in history, remained unconvinced until he was shown a computer simulation demonstrating the predicted result."[37]*

That's an example of how powerful our innate biases can be. Even in the face of solid evidence that our thinking is incorrect, we persist in our common-sense beliefs.

## BEHAVIORAL BIASES MAY APPLY TO OTHERS—BUT I'M TOO SMART FOR THAT

We have said earlier that behavioral biases and the limitations of common sense have nothing to do with intelligence. We mean this in the sense that we are all inherently bound by the same biases and

---

36  *Marilyn vos Savant, "Ask Marilyn," Parade Magazine, Sept. 9, 1990a, p. 16. Available at http://marilynvossavant.com/game-show-problem/*

37  John Tierney, "Behind Monty Hall's Doors: Puzzle, Debate, and Answer?" *New York Times*, July 21, 1991, accessed 2018, https://www.nytimes.com/1991/07/21/us/behind-monty-hall-s-doors-puzzle-debate-and-answer.html; Andrew Vazsonyi, "The Real-Life Adventures of a Decision Scientist: Which Door Has the Cadillac?" *Decision Line*, December/January 1998-1999, accessed 2018, https://web.archive.org/web/20140413131827/http://www.decisionsciences.org/DecisionLine/Vol30/30_1/vazs30_1.pdf.

errors of mental reasoning that Kahneman and Tversky first documented in the 1960s.

It's interesting to note however that a new study in the *Journal of Personality and Social Psychology* led by Richard West at James Madison University and Keith Stanovich at the University of Toronto suggests that, in many instances, *"smarter people are more vulnerable to these thinking errors."*[38] Although we assume that intelligence is a buffer against bias—that's why those with higher SAT scores think they are less prone to these universal thinking mistakes—it can actually be a subtle curse. "Ouch!" say those who think themselves too smart for their thinking to be compromised by behavioral biases.

West goes on to say that "perhaps our most dangerous bias is that we naturally assume that everyone else is more susceptible to thinking errors, a tendency known as the 'bias blind spot.' This is rooted in our ability to spot systematic mistakes in the decisions of others—we excel at noticing the flaws of friends—and our inability to spot those same mistakes in ourselves. We readily forgive our own minds but look harshly upon the minds of other people."

And here's the unsettling punch line: "Intelligence seems to make things worse. This trend held for many of the specific biases, indicating that smarter people (at least as measured by SAT scores) and those more likely to engage in deliberation were slightly more vulnerable to common mental mistakes."

## BEHAVIORAL BIASES AND INVESTING

If you do an Internet search for "behavioral biases" or "cognitive biases," you will find that research has identified and documented more than one hundred of them. Our point in the following section

---

38   Lehrer, "Why Smart People Are Stupid, " emphasis added.

is not to discuss them all. Instead, it is to give readers a flavor for the common biases that have been identified in academic research and how they affect our investment decision-making.

## Recency Bias

Doug and Kathy are both seventy-five years old. For many years, Doug was a small business owner. As they moved closer to retirement, Doug started to focus more on their personal finances. He regretted some of the decisions he'd made in the past and wanted to be very conscientious moving forward. He didn't want to take a lot of risk, but he also didn't want to give up returns by lagging the stock market. In other words, he wanted to have his cake and eat it, too. He thought financial markets at the time were starting to look risky. To allay his concerns, their advisor moved much of their stock allocation into bonds to reduce risk. It was a sound strategy designed to respond to his growing unease with financial market conditions.

Despite Doug's concerns and his move to a more conservative portfolio, nothing bad happened in the stock market. Instead, it soared and his portfolio lagged the market. Lagging the market bothered him—a lot. All he could think about was how much money he could have made had he invested everything in stocks.

He continually compared the returns of his defensive portfolio with the returns of index funds that mirrored the S&P 500. Every time he opened his monthly statements, he was reminded of how much money he could have been making. He finally decided he could do better himself, and so took more than $1 million from his portfolio into his own hands to invest in various stock funds.

It turned out that Doug had been right to be concerned about financial markets, but just a little premature with his concerns. The economy eventually entered recession, and he watched as his stock portfolio dropped 30 percent, then 40 percent, and finally more than 50 percent from its peak. It turned out that his defensive portfolio would have weathered the storm, and avoiding the recession losses would have more than made up for missing some returns. However, as long as the stock market was doing well, all he could think about was the returns he wasn't getting, and he ultimately paid the price.

Doug's actions are an example of *recency bias*. It's a mental shortcut in which investors extrapolate recent events into the future indefinitely. For example, Bloomberg surveys market strategists on a weekly basis and asks for their recommended portfolio weightings of stocks, bonds, and cash. The highest recommended percent of stocks came just after the peak of the Internet bubble in 2000, that is, when the market was at its highest. The lowest recommended percent of stocks came just after the lows of the 2008 financial crisis. In effect, analysts are collectively making recommendations that are nothing more than extrapolations of what has happened recently. If stocks have been doing poorly, they advise against owning them. If stocks have been doing great, they advise to buy them.

Here is another example of recency bias in action. An individual with two investments looks at the one that has performed better over the last two years and says, "It's just basic common sense to sell the low performer and buy the high performer." We know from experience that the recency bias is the most pervasive in all of investing. If you asked one hundred people which investment they would choose (the low performer or the high performer), nearly 100 percent will choose the investment that did the best most recently, no questions asked. We have done this experiment many times and the results are always the same.

Individual investors aren't the only ones guilty of recency bias. Early in his career, Richard was a loan officer with Continental Bank, the largest bank in Chicago. Oil and gas prices were soaring at the time, and Continental was deeply involved in oil and gas lending. His bank began to aggressively buy oil and gas loans from other banks. They bought a huge number of loans from the Penn Square Bank in Oklahoma City. You may recall that Penn Square Bank failed, and Continental Bank collapsed into a $4.5 billion federal government bailout.

Every January, *Money Magazine* lists the top ten stock mutual funds from the previous year. The reason: people want to invest in the funds that have done well recently. This is a classic example of recency bias and *Money Magazine* knows what consumers want. It's also well established in the mutual fund industry that new investments into and redemptions from investment funds follow performance. If a fund posts big returns one year, then investors flock to invest. If a fund posts poor returns, investors flee. That's recency bias.

Recency bias originates from our innate human tendency to extrapolate the recent past into the future. Our thinking is greatly influenced by what has happened recently. We weigh recent events more heavily in our thinking, even though there is no rational basis for that assumption. In other words, without really thinking it through, we make a quick decision based on an underlying belief that the future will look like the past. Therefore, if an investment was better last year or the last two years or even the last five years, we think it will also be better in the future.

In chapter 2 we saw that individual investors oversimplify a complex problem and therefore end up choosing the wrong investment. We noted two elements missing from their thinking, and it's the missing elements that make all the difference. The first is an understanding of the power of minimizing losses. Controlling losses affects portfolio growth far more than maximizing gains. The second is failure to understand that the business cycle drives nearly all investment risk and return.

We often say the only returns that matter for long-term investors are those earned over the complete business cycle. It does an investor no good to earn high returns during good economic times, only to lose it all in the next recession. That makes the entire business cycle the relevant period of time for evaluating any investment strategy rather than some arbitrary fixed calendar period, such as last year, last two years, last five years, etc.

Of course, the problem with that idea is it makes decision-making harder, and we human beings naturally like decisions to be easy. There is no fixed calendar period for the business cycle. As noted in chapter 4, the historical average for economic expansions is five years, but the longest on record was ten years. They start and end when they start and end, and the beginning and end of the business cycle has nothing to do with calendar periods. Additionally, when you open your investment statements, you have probably noticed there is nothing about the business cycle provided in their reporting. Nobody is compiling that information for individual investors, and that makes it hard to evaluate investment performance.

Nonetheless, that's the reality of how financial markets and investment portfolios work. There is always a business cycle with both large gains and large losses, and controlling losses matters far more for portfolio performance than maximizing gains. This means we must be aware of our natural recency bias in order to keep it from leading us astray.

## Confirmation Bias

We like to think that our opinions result from years of rational, objective analysis and the careful gathering and evaluation of facts and data before reaching a conclusion. However, research shows that we usually reach conclusions first and then search for and recall information that supports our preexisting beliefs.

For example, if an investor thinks the future of the economy is gloomy, they tend to read news sources and listen to pundits that support that point of view. In other words, whether they realize it or not, they are selectively exposing themselves to information and opinions that support what they already believe.

We have observed that many investors have their favorite sources for financial news. Some subscribe to newsletters that have a strong point of view about what's going to happen in the future. It's clear that these investors have sought out news sources with angles consistent with what they already believe. If an investor believes a period of gloom is coming, rather than approaching the problem by saying, "I want information on all the different points of view," they find sources that confirm their gloomy outlook.

A few months ago, a physician and his wife reached out to us for advice. He already owned a fair amount of gold and silver and saw those investments as protection. However, those investments hadn't done well recently, and he was considering our services. Had we said, "You're so wise to be holding gold and silver and you probably need even more of it," it's likely he would have signed on as a client. However, we didn't share his view and didn't jump on his bandwagon. He elected to continue looking for an investment advisor because it turned out what he really wanted was validation in the form of confirmation of his existing beliefs, not independent advice.

We see confirmation bias at work in our choice of where to get our news. Some people watch *Fox News* not because they want to be exposed to the whole spectrum of political ideas, but because they want to hear news presented in a way that's consistent with how they view the world. Likewise, people with a more left-leaning political point of view prefer to read the *New York Times* for the same reason.

## Optimism Bias

Remember Lake Wobegon? It was Garrison Keillor's fictitious town where all the women are good-looking, all the men are strong, and all the children are above average. Research has shown that we live in a Lake Wobegon world where we indulge our natural human tendency to over-estimate our achievements and capabilities in relation to others. For example, more than ninety percent of college professors believe they have above-average teaching skills.[39] Seventy percent of high school students claim to have above-average leadership skills.[40] Ninety-three percent of drivers say their driving skills are above average.[41]

In Doug and Kathy's story, Doug is an example of the optimism bias because he greatly overestimated his understanding of the portfolio investment problem.

## Loss Aversion

It's human nature to be risk-averse. Research has shown that we experience losses at two-and-a-half times the rate of equivalent

---

39   K. Patricia Cross, "Not can, but *will* college teaching be improved?" *New Directions for Higher Education* 1977, no. 17 (Spring 1977): 1–15, https://doi.org/10.1002/he.36919771703.

40   Alex Mayyasi, "Why Do We All Think We're Above Average?" Priceonomics, July 17, 2013, https://priceonomics.com/why-do-we-all-think-were-above-average/.

41   Ola Svenson, "Are we all less risky and more skillful than our fellow drivers?" *Acta Psychological* 42, no. 2 (February 1981): 143–148, https://doi.org/10.1016/0001-6918(81)90005-6.

gains.[42] In other words, the pain from losing $100 is two-and-a-half times greater than the pleasure of gaining $100. Classic behavioral economics suggests that, if we were completely rational beings, we would evaluate these possibilities as being equal. Gaining or losing would be a 50/50 proposition. We would place the same value on the potential of a $100 gain as a $100 loss. Instead, we view the potential of a $100 loss as two-and-a-half times more painful than a $100 gain. Therefore, researchers conclude that investors are not perfectly rational—they are instead loss-averse.

There is no doubt that humans are naturally loss-averse. For example, imagine you are at the office in the break room getting coffee, and you overhear your boss saying he wants to give you a $400 per month raise. You are happy. Now consider the opposite situation. You overhear your boss talking to the HR manager about cutting your salary by $400 per month. Obviously, you are unhappy, and your unhappiness is probably much greater about the salary reduction than is your happiness at the prospect of a raise.

Where we part company with the classic interpretation of loss aversion is the conclusion that it's irrational. In the raise/pay cut example, the negative impact to the household budget of losing $400 per month is probably much greater than the positive impact of gaining an additional $400 for new spending. In one case it may make the difference in being able to pay the utility bill (salary reduction) versus being able to go out for dinner more often (salary increase). It's hard to see that as being irrational. When it comes to investing, we think investors' loss-averse instincts are actually pointing them in the right direction. One of the key points we have been making in

---

42   Richard H. Thaler, Amos Tversky, Daniel Kahneman, and Alan Schwarts, "The Effect of Myopia and Loss Aversion on Risk Taking: An Experimental Test," *Quarterly Journal of Economics* (May 1997): 647–661.

this book is that avoiding losses matters far more than getting all the gains. This is just the basic math of portfolio dynamics.

## Herding Bias

*Herding bias* refers to the tendency for individuals to mimic the actions, whether rational or irrational, of a larger group. Humans are biologically wired to run in herds, which can be large or small, bullish or bearish. It reflects the social pressure to conform. Most people have a natural desire to be accepted by the group rather than be branded an outsider. This behavior was necessary when being part of the social group was important to survival. An outcast in ancestral times would have been in trouble. Today, this manifests in a natural desire to be accepted by the social group rather than to be branded an outcast. Following the herd is an ideal way of becoming a member.

Herding also reflects our tendency to believe that the group is unlikely to be wrong. One may be skeptical about a particular idea, suspecting it may be irrational or incorrect, but most people will still follow the herd.

A classic example of herd behavior occurred in the late 1990s when investors poured enormous amounts of money into the stocks of young Internet companies even though many of them weren't making profits and were unlikely to generate significant revenues in the foreseeable future. This created a technology stock bubble, which led to a technology stock bubble collapse.

While the technology bubble lasted, some investors were getting 70–80 percent returns. Investors were bombarded with news of high-flying Internet stocks; all the hype was about dotcom stocks. This was a perfect example of herding: almost everyone was doing one thing and anyone who wasn't participating wanted on the bandwagon. It's also an example of recency bias: because share prices were rising in the recent past, they expected them to keep rising in the future.

## BIASES AT WORK

In chapter 3 we referenced Dalbar Inc., the financial community's leading independent expert for evaluating, auditing, and rating business practices. Dalbar has been producing its *Quantitative Analysis of Investor Behavior* (QAIB) studies since 1994. In 2016, its twenty-second *Annual Quantitative Analysis of Investor Behavior* talked about the causes, evidence, and consequences of poor investment decisions.[43] Essentially, it stated that the average investor's performance is weak because he or she gets in late, is reactive to short-term market conditions, and doesn't stay invested long enough to participate in market expansion. This is something we see over and over in the lives of individual investors.

## *Paul's Story*

Paul is a senior financial manager who works for a large corporation. He earned an MBA at a top graduate school of business and is very analytical. He is a do-it-yourself investor but came to see us about a year ago because he was interested in considering our investment strategies.

Paul invests primarily in stock mutual funds and has a straightforward strategy for managing his portfolio. Each year on December 31, he looks at the past year's performance of each fund he owns. He

---

43   DALBAR, *22nd Annual Quantitative Analysis of Investor Behavior for Period Ended 12/31/2015*, 2016, www.qidllc.com/wp-content/uploads/2016/02/2016-Dalbar-QAIB-Report.pdf.

then replaces the poorest-performing funds with other funds that did better over the same period.

Paul's investment strategy is apparently quite common. YiLi Chien, a senior economist at the Federal Reserve Bank of St. Louis, did a study of the relationship between stock mutual fund performance and *fund flows*, meaning new investments and redemptions from mutual funds.[44] He found that equity mutual fund flows correlated positively with past returns. In other words, investors collectively tend to withdraw money from mutual funds that did worse in the recent past and invest new money in funds that did well, just like Paul.

Paul has no desire to spend a lot of time doing analysis, and his strategy seemed like basic common sense to him. He is a highly competent business manager and explained his strategy this way: "In my organization we are constantly evaluating how everyone is doing. If expenses are running too high, we take action to bring them back into line. If we have an employee who is not getting the job done, then we are quick to make a change. I use the same approach in managing my portfolio. I keep the winners and I fire the losers. That's how I run my business and it's also how I run my investment portfolio."[45]

That's good hard-nosed business thinking. Paul is very good at his job, and it seems to him basic common sense that the same approach that makes him successful in business will make him successful in investing. That would be true if business management and portfolio management were similar, but they are not.

---

44   YiLi Chien, "Chasing Returns Has a High Cost for Investors," On the Economy blog, April 14, 2014, www.stlouisfed.org/on-the-economy/2014/april/chasing-returns-has-a-high-cost-for-investors

45   Personal communication, July 20, 2017.

For example, when Paul "fires" his less successful mutual funds and replaces them with funds that did better over the same period, he is implicitly assuming that what happened in the past will recur in the future. The "good" funds will continue their "good" performance and the "poor" funds will do likewise.

## Mean-Reversion

This idea often makes sense in business. If the division's expenses are running too high in the recent past, that condition will usually persist into the future unless something is done to correct the problem. Therefore, it's prudent to look at last year's results. Likewise, if an employee isn't getting the job done, you are likely to see more of the same in the future unless a change is made.

However, financial markets don't work the same way. In fact, they often work in ways opposite from our common-sense expectations. YiLi Chien, in the study previously referenced, wondered whether investors following Paul's strategy were better off, worse off, or about the same in comparison to the market average. Chien found that switching from lesser-performing funds to better-performing funds each year caused investors to do worse by about 2 percent per year. That may not sound like much, but if your average returns are around 6 percent, that means your results are 33 percent worse with this strategy.

The reason for this outcome is a statistical concept known as *mean-reversion*. The tendency is for higher-performing funds to mean-revert to lower performance in the next year. The reverse is also true for lower-performing funds. This is exactly the opposite of what one would expect in the business world, and is contrary to our common sense understanding of how the investment world works.

In chapter 2 we showed that the low-volatility strategy earned about $1.8 million more in profit than the S&P 500 did over a sixteen-year period on an original $1 million investment. However, that analysis assumed an investor earned the same return as the S&P 500. Based on Chien's study, if investors surrendered an additional 2 percent in return each year simply by following Paul's strategy of switching to higher-performing funds, they would give up an additional $400,000 of profit over the same period. That gives the low-volatility strategy an advantage of $2.2 million in comparison to the strategy of a typical stock investor.

One question we asked Paul was whether he considered the risk profile of his mutual funds when evaluating their past performance. In other words, had he considered the possibility that funds with higher returns in the past year may have achieved those returns by taking more risk? That was not something he had considered, and he wasn't quite sure how to go about it. However, it's easy to see that if you are selecting mutual funds based on higher recent returns without any consideration of the risk, then it's likely that you will end up with more risk in your portfolio. We doubt that's the objective Paul had in mind.

What about the business cycle? We have made the point that risk and return are driven by the business cycle, and the only returns that matter for long-term investors are those earned over the complete cycle. Where is the business cycle in Paul's investment strategy? Once again, just like consideration of risk, it's missing in action.

## Framing

A major part of the problem Paul is facing has to do with another behavioral bias known as *framing*. This means that people tend to reach conclusions based on the framework within which the problem is presented. For example, here is a summary of a classic study done on framing.

Amos Tversky and Daniel Kahneman explored how different phrasing affected participants' responses to a mathematically equivalent choice in a hypothetical life and death situation in 1981. Participants were asked to choose between two treatments for six hundred people affected by a deadly disease. Treatment A was predicted to result in four hundred deaths, whereas Treatment B had a 33 percent chance that no one would die but a 66 percent chance that everyone would die. This choice was then presented to participants either with positive framing, i.e. how many people would live, or with negative framing, i.e. how many people would die.

| FRAMING | TREATMENT A | TREATMENT B |
|---------|-------------|-------------|
| Positive | "Saves two hundred lives" | "33 percent chance of saving all six hundred people; 66 percent chance of saving no one." |
| Negative | "Four hundred people will die" | "33 percent chance that no one will die; 66 percent chance that all six hundred will die." |

Treatment A was chosen by 72 percent of participants when it was presented with positive framing (save two hundred lives), but it was chosen by only 22 percent of participants when the same choice was presented with negative framing (four hundred people will die). Simply changing how the information was presented dramatically changed the decisions people made.[46]

---

46  A. Tversky, and D. Kahneman, "The framing of decisions and the psychology of choice," *SCIENCE* 4481, no. 211 (January 30, 1981): 453–458, https://doi.org/10.1126/science.7455683.

In Paul's case, he is not only taking a common-sense approach to his portfolio strategy by "keeping the winners and firing the losers," his thinking is also reinforced by the typical presentation of the information assumed to be relevant to making an informed investment decision.

Below is a typical performance profile for the Fidelity Contra Fund (FCNTX) taken from a well-known source that compiles data for mutual fund investors.[47] We selected the Contra Fund at random because it's a large, well-known fund. It doesn't matter which fund you select. What matters is understanding the information that's typically presented to investors for investment decision-making and the extent to which it's relevant to the investment decision.

| History (12/31/2017) | 2012 | 2013 | 2014 | 2015 | 2016 | 2017 |
|---|---|---|---|---|---|---|
| FCNTX | 16.26 | 34.15 | 9.56 | 6.46 | 3.36 | 32.26 |
| S&P 500 TR USD | 16.00 | 32.39 | 13.69 | 1.38 | 11.96 | 21.83 |
| Category (LG) | 15.34 | 33.92 | 10.00 | 3.60 | 3.23 | 27.67 |
| +/– S&P 500 TR USD | 0.25 | 1.76 | -4.13 | 5.08 | -8.60 | 10.43 |
| +/– Category (LG) | 0.92 | 0.23 | -0.44 | 2.86 | 0.14 | 4.60 |
| Annual Report Net Expense Ratio | 0.66 | 0.64 | 0.70 | 0.68 | – | – |
| Turnover Ratio | 46 | 45 | 35 | 41 | – | – |
| Rank in Category | 36 | 46 | 56 | 27 | 48 | 21 |
| Fund Category | LG | LG | LG | LG | LG | LG |

What we see in this profile are the yearly returns for the fund and its comparison to the S&P 500—peers in the same category—and fund expenses. This presentation of data on past performance is typical of what is provided in sales literature, websites, and prospectuses across the investment industry. There is nothing wrong with the information, as far as it goes. The real question is whether it provides the information we need to make a sound investment decision.

---

47 "Fidelity® Contrafund® Fund," Morningstar, http://performance.morningstar.com/fund/performance-return.action?t=FCNTX.

For example, it's nice to know that FCNTX had a return of 32 percent versus 22 percent for the S&P 500 in 2017. Obviously, 32 percent is higher than 22 percent, but is 32 percent "better" than 22 percent? The answer to that question depends on how much risk the fund takes to generate its returns. If FCNTX has about the same risk as the S&P 500 or even less, then 32 percent for FCNTX versus 22 percent for the S&P 500 is a great result. However, if FCNTX has twice the risk of the S&P 500, then 32 percent is a poor result. Unfortunately, we don't know which because there is no information provided about risk. It's impossible to tell whether FCNTX is better than the S&P 500, because critical information about risk is missing.

What about the business cycle? What is the relevance of knowing year-by-year returns for 2012 through 2017? Very little that we can see. This series of returns is irrelevant and may even be misleading for making a sound investment decision. Here is why.

As mentioned earlier, the expansion phase of the current business cycle began in 2009 and continues in 2018 as we write. Therefore, all we have in the presentation above are returns for six years during the expansion phase of the current business cycle. One of the lessons from the low-volatility effect was that returns during the expansion phase tell us nothing about how the investment performs over the complete cycle. In fact, in the low-volatility example, focusing on recent expansion-phase returns is what leads most everyone to the *wrong conclusion* when it comes to selecting the better investment strategy.

Therefore, there are two key pieces of information necessary to evaluate one investment versus another: (1) risk, and (2) return over the complete business cycle—neither of which are provided. The information provided is insufficient, and the information critical to the decision is missing. No wonder individual investors have a hard time.

This brings us back to the framing bias. Individual investors tend to reach conclusions based on the framework within which the problem is presented. It's human nature to work with the information presented rather than think about what information may be missing and whether that information would make a difference. Mutual fund companies provide annual returns for the past five years, and people tend to regard that as the information relevant to the decision. If other information were necessary, people assume it would have been provided. That's an irrational assumption.

Behavioral biases have nothing to do with intelligence. They are hard-wired in all of us. Unfortunately, they result in simplistic decision rules that often lead us astray as investors. The greatest obstacle to becoming a better investor is not technical mastery, it is how we think.

# CHAPTER 6

# RETHINKING THE STANDARD MODEL

*Ferdinand Magellan set out in five ships* in 1519, believing he could reach the East by sailing west from Spain to Asia. The result was the discovery of the Pacific Ocean and, as we were taught in elementary school, definitive proof that the earth is round. However, nearly 1,800 years before Magellan, the ancient Greeks deduced that the earth is round by comparing the shadows of sticks in different locations. When the sun was directly overhead, one of the sticks would not cast a shadow. However, a stick of equal length placed in a distant location at the same time of day, say five hundred miles away, did cast a shadow.

The Greeks reasoned that if the earth was flat, then both sticks would cast the same shadow because they would be positioned at the same angle to the sun. However, if the length of the shadows was different, the only possible explanation was that the sticks were at different angles to the sun. This meant the earth was curved. They went on to use the difference in the length of the shadows to calculate the circumference of the earth and came up with an answer very close to that shown by our present-day calculations. Not bad for 250 BC.

## WHAT DOES "YOU CAN'T TIME THE MARKET" REALLY MEAN?

Despite the cleverness of the Greeks, it's easy to see how ancient people believed the earth was flat. There are very good reasons why the earth seems flat. It has to do with a concept called *local flatness*. Any object can appear flat if you zoom in close enough. The earth is immense in relation to the size of human beings, and in that context, we are just zoomed in really close.

We were born and raised on the Great Plains. We have seen plenty of flat land that stretches as far as the eye can see. Our description of the land as flat is true, but that doesn't mean we think the earth is flat. We know there is an unseen curvature that escapes our perception. Our statement about flat land is not true when carried to an extreme.

Similarly, the 2013 Nobel Prizes in Economics recalled an example of ideas that may be true in their intended context but may not be true when extended more broadly. One of the recipients that year was Eugene Fama of the University of Chicago. Fama is often referred to as the "father of modern finance." He is best known for his empirical work on portfolio theory and asset pricing, and is strongly identified with the oft-repeated advice to individual investors: "You can't time the market." How should we think about that statement and what does it really mean for investing? We'll need to unpack it a bit to answer those questions.

The 2013 Nobel Prize Committee succinctly summarized Fama's work as follows: "Beginning in the 1960s, Fama and several collaborators demonstrated that stock prices are extremely difficult to predict in the short run, and that new information is very quickly incorporated into prices."[48] In other words, Fama showed there is no reliable way to predict the price of stocks and bonds over the next few days or weeks. We think that is exactly right. Any investment strategy premised on the ability to predict near-term security prices is a fool's errand. On that basis, it is true to say, "You can't time the market."

However, we often see that idea extended far beyond its original context to become an all-encompassing worldview about managing investment portfolios. This takes the form of statements such as: "You can't time the market. Therefore, your only choice is to buy and hold a passive, static portfolio." In this context, the idea is broadly extended to suggest that it is impossible to ever know anything useful about market conditions that would provide a basis for changing one's portfolio. But has that been proven to be true? Quite the contrary, as Robert Shiller of Yale University established twenty years after Fama's work.

It is ironic that Shiller shared the 2013 Nobel Prize with Fama. In announcing the recipients of the prize, the Nobel Committee said, "If prices are nearly impossible to predict over days or weeks (as Fama showed), then shouldn't they be even harder to predict over several years? The answer is no, as Robert Shiller discovered in the early 1980s."[49] Shiller's findings challenged the widely accepted theory of efficient markets and set off a revolution in finance and investment

---

48   Nobel Foundation, "2013 Nobel Prize in Economics: Trendspotting in Asset Markets," *ScienceDaily*, Oct. 14, 2013, https://www.sciencedaily.com/releases/2013/10/131014082140.htm.

49   Nobel Foundation, "2013 Nobel Prize in Economics: Trendspotting."

management. He showed that financial market conditions are predictive of future returns and risk.

In chapter 3 we discussed the Standard Industry Investment Model, or the Standard Model. We coined that term because the standard advice given to individual investors by the investment advice industry is based on some version of that model. The Standard Model takes a passive approach to portfolio management by prescribing an unchanging allocation among investment assets. In other words, portfolio holdings are always the same, no matter the conditions. We noted there are important advantages to following the Standard Model. It has been consistently shown that individual investors making decisions on their own underperform the results of following the Standard Model.

But, saying the Standard Model is better than the decisions individuals make on their own is not the same as saying it is the best way to manage an investment portfolio. There have been many advances documented in published academic research over the past thirty years that are not reflected in the Standard Model. Not the least of these are Shiller's insights noted previously that investment conditions matter and have much to tell us about future risk and return.

In the next section, we'll review the insights we've been discussing so far in this book. Then we will consider what the insights suggest about an alternative approach to the portfolio management problem.


## RECAP OF INSIGHTS

### Standard Industry Investment Model

In chapter 3 we noted that the Standard Model is based on an important set of ideas in Modern Portfolio Theory (MPT). The

Standard Model and MPT assume that risk is a constant and that large losses arise randomly. This means the risk of any asset class is assumed to be the same under all conditions. It also means that large losses randomly originate from some unknown source and could appear at any moment.

Because risk is assumed to be constant and random, the Standard Model prescribes that your portfolio should always be the same. In constructing investment portfolios, the Standard Model also assumes a constant long-term relationship between portfolio returns and portfolio risk. In other words, if you are willing to hold a riskier portfolio, then you will be rewarded with higher returns.

However, our research has shown that risk is not constant and random. Instead, the business cycle drives investment risk and, as a result, risk is neither constant nor random. In addition, there is not a constant relationship between portfolio returns and portfolio risk. Over the last ninety years, 60 percent of the time a higher-risk portfolio has not rewarded investors with higher returns. In summary, two key underlying assumptions of the Standard Model which is used throughout the investment advice industry to design investment portfolios are not true.

## Business Cycle

In chapters 3 and 4, we demonstrated that the business cycle drives risk and return in financial markets. Risk is not constant and random (as assumed by the Standard Model and MPT) because it is driven by the business cycle.

Investment risk is low when the economy is expanding, and risk is high when the economy enters recession. Even Fama (along with

Ken French of Dartmouth) acknowledged this in a 1989 paper documenting the impact of the business cycle on returns and risk.[50]

The chart below shows that the risk of holding stocks depends primarily on the business cycle. Solid periods represent growth in the economy while dashed periods are recessions when the economy is shrinking.

### S&P 500 Adjusted for Inflation

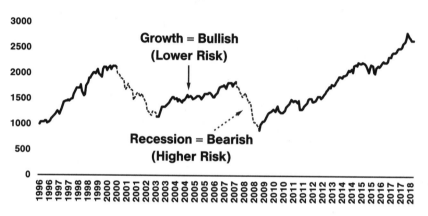

This is the key insight that changes everything in comparison to the Standard Model. Because the Standard Model assumes that stock risk is constant, always high, and completely random, portfolios are typically underinvested in stocks during times of economic growth and overinvested in stocks during recessions. Because they are underinvested when the economy is growing, they sacrifice portfolio growth, and because they are overinvested during recessions, they sustain large losses.

The business cycle is the most important factor determining risk and return in an investment portfolio, but it's missing from the Standard Model and MPT.

---

50  Eugene F. Fama and Kenneth R. French, "Business Conditions and Expected Returns on Stocks and Bonds," *Journal of Financial Economics* 25, (1989): 23–49.

## Investment Conditions

Investment conditions matter because they tell us about the future course of investment returns and risk. It was for this insight that Shiller was recognized with the 2013 Nobel Prize in Economic Sciences. However, despite their demonstrated importance, investment conditions are missing from the Standard Model and MPT.

## Asset Allocation

Research published in 2000 by Ibbotson and Kaplan found that 90–100 percent of the risk and return performance of a portfolio is determined by the percentage allocation among the major asset classes, such as stocks and bonds.[51] This means that nearly all portfolio risk and return is determined by asset allocation, and very little is determined by the individual securities you (or your mutual fund manager) select within each asset class. *Another way of saying this is the only thing that moves the needle in terms of portfolio outcomes (risk and return) is changing the percentage allocation between stocks and bonds.*

This is well recognized in the Standard Model and MPT, which adjusts the percentage of stocks and bonds depending on the investor's risk tolerance and need for growth. If you need growth and are willing to tolerate higher risk, then you should hold a high percentage in stocks and relatively few bonds. If you want lower risk and are willing to sacrifice portfolio growth, then you should hold a low percentage of the portfolio in stocks. *However, once the allocation is determined, the Standard Model is passive.* The allocation between

---

51  Roger G. Ibbotson and Paul D. Kaplan, "Does Asset Allocation Policy Explain 40, 90, or 100 Percent of Performance?" *CFA Institute Publications*, https://doi. org/10.2469/faj.v56.n1.2327.

stocks and bonds is held constant, no matter what the investment conditions.

However, we know from Shiller that investment conditions matter and can be understood. We have also seen that risk and return vary greatly depending on conditions (bullish versus bearish). We saw in chapter 1 that bullish conditions contain most of the returns for stocks and relatively low risk while bearish conditions have paltry returns and very high risk. We know there is always a business cycle which can be understood and measured, and which drives nearly all risk and return. Finally, we know from Ibbotson and Kaplan that asset allocation determines nearly all risk and return in a portfolio. When you put it all together, does it make sense to be passive about asset allocation in a portfolio? Clearly, it does not.

## Future Risk and Return

We know future returns over the next seven to ten years will be poor and risk will be high for portfolios following the Standard Model. It's true that conditions are currently very favorable for stocks and these conditions could continue for another year or two, with attractive gains. But we also know that large stock losses will occur sooner rather than later because stock prices are at historically high levels and corporate profit margins are the highest ever. No one knows the timing of the next recession. Nevertheless, as shown in the following chart, business cycles don't last forever, and we are in the late innings of the current expansion.

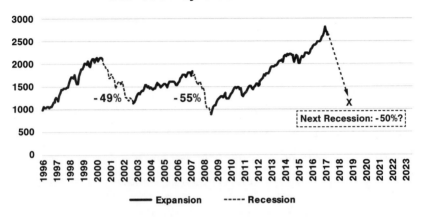

**S&P 500 Adjusted for Inflation**

Next Recession: -50%?

-49%     -55%     X

— Expansion     ----- Recession

We also know we are at the end or near the end of the long bull market in bond returns. Interest rates have been falling for thirty-six years and because of this bond returns have been extraordinary over that period. This is because falling interest rates boost bond returns. We don't know whether future interest rates will remain at their current low levels or will move higher, and neither does anyone else. If they remain low, that would be the scenario that has played out in Japan over the last thirty years, and it is possible we will follow the same path. Or, perhaps interest rates will go higher as many predict.

Neither scenario will be kind to bond investors. Interest rates are close to five thousand-year lows today. Rates may go higher, or they may stay the same, but they can't go much lower. This means future bond returns are destined to be very low, that is, much lower than they have been over the past forty years. This is just basic financial math. Yet, most portfolios, financial plans, and conventional wisdom follow the Standard Model's recommendation of a passive bond allocation of 40 percent or more in the portfolio, with the percentage of bonds increasing with age.

A common rule of thumb suggests a bond allocation equal to your age. Therefore, if you are age fifty, bonds should be 50 percent of your portfolio and stocks the other 50 percent. If you are age seventy, bonds should be 70 percent. By now you know to beware of so-called "rules of thumb" because they are heuristic shortcuts and usually wrong. This rule of thumb is no exception. The conventional wisdom of investment portfolios assumes a continuation of the extraordinary bond returns of the last thirty-six years which was driven by falling interest rates. As noted above, that is impossible.

## Importance of Controlling Losses

Controlling losses matters far more than maximizing gains in determining portfolio results. This was one of the lessons from the low-volatility effect. Another lesson was that it's possible to get consistently better returns with less risk over the complete business cycle by mitigating recession losses. This is exactly the opposite of what is assumed by the Standard Model and MPT.

> *Controlling losses matters far more than maximizing gains in determining portfolio results.*

As we discussed earlier, recession losses are the primary reason future returns will be poor and risk will be high for portfolios that are following the Standard Model. The best way to improve portfolio returns and reduce risk is to avoid recession losses. We know there will be a recession sooner rather than later.

A common mistake is to think large losses don't matter if you have the stomach to hang on through the losses. After all, stock prices eventually recover and go higher, right?

Setting aside the emotional distress of seeing your life savings reduced by one-third or more (which is more than most people can stand), it's true that stock prices eventually recover to their former levels after the recession. However, that process does not occur overnight. It commonly takes six to seven years to get back to even. That's a very long period with a 0 percent return in one's portfolio. That's an enormous opportunity cost versus an approach which mitigates the losses.

The important question is not whether your portfolio will eventually return to its pre-recession level. Rather, the question is where your portfolio might be had you avoided the recession losses.

The problem of large recession losses is exacerbated when you consider the impact of withdrawing from the portfolio to fund retirement living expenses. If you are withdrawing from the portfolio, even if stocks recover, your portfolio may never recover in terms of supporting the withdrawals you'd been planning. Avoiding losses becomes even more important if you are approaching or in retirement. The following chart illustrates the math:

## Illustration: The Surprising Path to Better Results

| Period | Type | S&P 500 Return | 80% of Return and Avoid Large Loss |
|--------|------|----------------|-----------------------------------|
| 2018 | Expansion | 15% | 12% |
| 2019 | Expansion | 12% | 10% |
| **2020** | **Recession** | **-50%** | **-5%** |
| 2021 | Expansion | 20% | 16% |
| 2022 | Expansion | 12% | 10% |
| 2023 | Expansion | 12% | 10% |
| Total Return | | -3% | +64% |

Recessions: Normal Part of the Business Cycle

In this chart, we have provided a hypothetical illustration of the impact of recession losses on portfolio returns. In one case, we assume a sequence of good stock returns in five out of six years, and a recession with large losses in one year. These returns and the recession loss are similar to what has happened historically. In the alternative, we assume an approach which earns only 80 percent of stock returns in the good years, but is able to hold recession losses to 5 percent. As you can see, the strategy that controls losses comes out way ahead, even though it lags most of the time. Controlling losses matters far more than getting all the gains in determining portfolio results.

## Behavioral Biases

Because the business cycle drives risk and return in financial markets, the complete cycle is the relevant period over which to judge investment returns and risk. It does an investor no good to earn high returns during the expansion phase of the business cycle, only to surrender those gains in the next recession.

However, our innate behavioral biases often lead us away from a better solution. Because we are naturally wired with these biases, it's not easy or natural to be a good investor. This is not so much because it's technically difficult; the principal obstacle is how we are accustomed to thinking about the problem.

As human beings, we are all prone to the biases discussed in chapter 5. However, the most insidious of these for individual investors is the *recency bias*. As we discussed, this bias leads us to judge portfolio outcomes based on shorter, recent periods of time even though the relevant period for long-term investors is the complete business cycle. In chapter 2, we showed that low-volatility stocks outperformed by a wide margin over two business cycles even though they lagged the S&P 500 78 percent of the time. We also saw this with the hypothetical illustration above in which the strategy with the superior outcome lagged significantly five out of six years. In both cases, the lesson is that avoiding losses matters far more than getting all the gains.

Active risk management is probabilistic. In chapter 1 we introduced the idea of probabilistic thinking and suggested it is the key to becoming a better investor. Nobody can accurately predict the course of financial markets in the short term. However, in chapter 1 we also showed that risk and return are not evenly distributed across financial market conditions. The likelihood of an unfavorable outcome is much higher when conditions are bearish. Therefore, it is smart to take defensive action when these conditions occur even if it turns out to be a false alarm. As a result, active management of risk will sometimes lag market benchmarks on a short-term basis.

Richard often tells clients about his experience growing up in Kansas to help them understand this idea. Kansas is well-known as part of the Midwest's "Tornado Alley." As a young boy, Richard was told to go to the basement with his family when tornado warnings sounded. Sometimes they even had the adventure of spending the night in the basement. Once the danger passed, the family would come up from the basement and resume their normal activities. Even though it was inconvenient to interrupt their activities and go to the basement, his parents knew it was the smart thing to do. Richard's home was never struck by a tornado, but his family never stopped going to the basement. Most of the time, tornado warnings expire without damage to structures. But not so with recessions; they are 100 percent certain to occur and do great damage to investment portfolios.

We're not suggesting that the objective in managing an investment portfolio should be to lag the market benchmarks most of the time. We are saying that if you sometimes lag because you are being attentive to and active about managing risk, being behind for a while doesn't matter. The important thing is to mitigate large losses. Mitigating losses is the thing that makes the biggest difference in the outcome of the portfolio over the whole cycle. This concept is counterintuitive. We're just not wired to think that way.

If we are to become better investors, part of the solution is to understand that we are prone to make these mistakes. Once we acknowledge our inherent predispositions, we can actively work to override our innate biases.

## Rethinking the Standard Model

Let's return to the metaphor we introduced earlier. Imagine a long road trip from San Francisco to Boston. The trip will take several days. You want to arrive as quickly as possible, but you also want to arrive safely. You know that getting there quickly and arriving safely are conflicting objectives. Along the way, you will encounter a variety of road conditions. Most of the time, conditions will be favorable with dry roads and sunny skies, but we may encounter heavy rain, sleet, snow, or ice.

If you are like most people, you know it makes sense to adjust your speed to the conditions you encounter. When skies are sunny and the road is dry, you will drive the speed limit or maybe even a bit faster. Even though you are driving fast, it's not risky because conditions are favorable. However, if you encounter snow and ice, the smart decision is to slow down. Conditions have become less favorable, and the risk of crashing has gone up.

When conditions go from bad to worse as we encounter a major winter storm, the smart decision is to exit the highway to avoid the risk of a serious accident. Even if you must get a room for the night and resume travel in the morning, you are more likely to arrive at your destination safely than if you try to drive through the storm.

This is a metaphor for the investing problem. We think it appropriately illustrates the central question investors are asking and need to ask: what is the best way to balance the conflicting objectives of arriving at our destination quickly and safely? The road trip metaphor contains several parallels to key ideas we've been discussing:

- Risk is not constant. This is because neither road conditions nor financial market conditions are constant.

- Conditions matter because they are the principal driver of risk.

- Road conditions are driven by the weather. Financial market conditions are driven by the business cycle.

- Slowing down when road conditions are risky is the best way to make sure you arrive at your destination safely and as quickly as possible. Likewise, controlling recession losses matters far more than maximizing gains in determining portfolio results.

Over the course of long-term investing, we know that conditions will vary from good to bad, and our major concern is crashing (i.e., the large losses that do major damage to portfolios). So, when skies are sunny and the road is dry, it makes sense to drive fast and hold more stocks. Even though we are driving fast, the risk of crashing is low because conditions are favorable.

When we encounter icy road conditions, it makes sense to slow down and cut back on stock exposure. Conditions have become less favorable and the risk of crashing has increased. When we encounter a major winter storm (recession), it makes sense to exit the highway and get a room for the night—that is, we should sell the remaining risky assets (stocks) and buy safety assets (government bonds). The next morning when the storm has passed and the roads are clear, we can reenter the highway (buy stocks) and resume driving fast.

We should note there are two other types of drivers on the road. One is the average investor, who is driving his portfolio by looking at what happened recently. We'll call him Mr. Recency Bias. He is barreling down the highway looking out the rear window. He slows down when he should be speeding up, and he speeds up when he should be slowing down. Of course, he has no chance of avoiding the icy road conditions we know are just ahead because all he sees is that the road behind is clear and dry.

The other driver on the road is Ms. Standard Model. She drives the whole route at the same speed using cruise control because the Standard Model prescribes that you always own the same investment assets in the same proportions regardless of conditions.

If you are very afraid of crashing (i.e., if you have low risk tolerance), then you are advised to set your cruise control at a low speed. This means your portfolio always holds few stocks and lots of bonds with a low expected return. Because your speed is always slow, you probably won't arrive at your destination on time, but your risk of crashing is less. However, even at a relatively slow speed, you may still crash or go in the ditch during a major winter storm. After all, the smartest strategy in those conditions is to pull off the road for the night.

On the other hand, if you are in a hurry and need portfolio growth to catch up, you are advised to set your cruise control at a high speed. This means you will hold more stocks and few bonds for a higher potential return, assuming you don't crash. However, because you are going fast all the time, you should expect to crash or go in the ditch when the winter storm descends. Which, after all, is the number-one thing you want to avoid in getting to your destination.

Here is perhaps the most important point we want to make in this book: It seems very logical that an investor would want to avoid a large crash, but, psychologically, it turns out to be easier for investors to think logically about driving than about investing.

When driving, we know it's smart to slow down when conditions worsen, even though other drivers are flying past us because they're ignoring the conditions. We've all had that happen, and some of us secretly hope to see those guys in the ditch farther down the road. However, even if they turn out to be fortunate and avoid crashing for the time being, we still know they're foolish. Just because they didn't crash (this time) doesn't mean we now think it's smart to drive eighty miles an hour when the roads are icy.

However, when it comes to investing (rather than driving), it's far more common for individual investors to lose sight of the bigger picture (i.e., avoiding crashes that are an inevitable part of the business cycle) and fall in line behind the crazy guy driving fast in the passing lane on icy roads. It turns out that this way of thinking is both bad news and good news.

The bad news is, because of our innate behavioral biases, we are not as logical about investing as we are about driving. Therefore, better investing requires awareness of our biases and the mistakes they cause us to make.

However, there is also good news, and the good news is very good indeed. The good news is that an opportunity for a better outcome exists. To seize that opportunity, however, we must consciously override our natural instincts plus turn a deaf ear to the investment advice industry's conventional wisdom. Doing this takes some measure of effort and courage. So, the "money" question all investors need to ask themselves is this: Am I committed to override my natural emotions and see the whole picture in order to be a better investor?

Bobby Jones, one of the greatest golfers of all time once said: "Competitive golf is played mainly on a six-inch course . . . the space between your ears." The same goes for investing—the biggest key to getting a better outcome is changing your thinking which requires mastering your natural instincts and emotions. If you can do that, you have a huge advantage over most investors and can profit greatly.

Our message is simple—no one can drive fast all the time and hope to avoid the large crash. In order to reduce the risk of crashing, we have to slow down as conditions worsen. Because you slow down for worsening conditions, it's inevitable that you will sometimes trail others who are driving in the fast lane—right up to the point where the large crash occurs. In the long run, being behind for a while doesn't matter. Remember the lesson from the low-volatility effect which came out miles ahead over the complete business cycle even though it trailed 78 percent of the time? Controlling losses matters far more than getting all the gains. You will finish far ahead by capturing your fair share of the gains while avoiding the inevitable large crash. That's the key to a better outcome.

# CHAPTER 7

# IMPLEMENTING ACTIVE RISK MANAGEMENT

*Jeff Bezos founded Amazon in 1994* and twenty-four years later has become the world's richest man. The company has expanded to a variety of products and services, including video and audio streaming and cloud infrastructure services, but his original idea was selling books online. At the time of Amazon's founding, book retailing in the US was dominated by Barnes & Nobel and Waldenbooks, with thousands of brick-and-mortar retail stores and 80 percent of the market. Bezos thought he had a better idea, but it required a different business model. Rather than building and operating traditional retail book stores, he invested in online technology and a network of distribution centers across the country. He started with a better idea and then built the specific business capabilities necessary to support that idea.

Twenty years ago, we began a process to improve our personal investing. We knew that the industry recommended passive, static portfolios with a constant allocation to stocks and other asset classes. However, we reached a different conclusion: asset class allocations should be actively managed, and portfolios should change as conditions change. *Because most of the activities of the investment advice industry are designed to provide passive rather than active management of risk, we realized that a different business model was necessary to provide an active management solution for our clients.*

What do we mean by "different business model?" A useful metaphor would be to compare a sandwich shop to a seafood restaurant. While both are in the business of preparing and serving food to their patrons, they require different activities and capabilities because there are important differences in the food they serve. Therefore, if you visited both kitchens, you would expect to find significant differences in the cooking equipment, recipes, ingredients, processes of food preparation, and skills of the employees. Likewise, *active management of portfolio risk requires a different business model than passive management.* The purpose of this chapter is to illustrate what it takes to implement active management by describing what you would find in the kitchen of our restaurant.

---

## THERE ARE EIGHT KEY ELEMENTS NECESSARY TO IMPLEMENT AN ACTIVE APPROACH TO MANAGING PORTFOLIO RISK AND RETURN:

1. Develop an objective, testable methodology to measure investment conditions.

2. Determine the best investment asset classes for each investment condition.

3. Design investment strategies and related trading rules.

4. Monitor and report investment conditions daily.

5. Implement and maintain a technology platform that supports active management.

6. Manage portfolios based on pre-defined, objective trading rules.

7. Hold low-cost, highly-liquid asset class investments (e.g., ETFs).

8. Maintain the discipline, commitment, and readiness to act every day, even though most days there is no need to act.

---

## 1. DEVELOP AN OBJECTIVE, TESTABLE METHODOLOGY TO MEASURE INVESTMENT CONDITIONS.

The first key to actively managing portfolio risk is developing an objective, testable methodology that allows you to measure investment conditions. We have said that portfolios should change as conditions change, but how do you know when conditions have changed? How do you even know what conditions are?

This is not a simple problem. We have been working for twenty years to design and refine how we measure conditions to have the information needed to know when changes are necessary in client portfolios. Our initial effort, based on what we call "economic indicators," was not completely successful.

We examined factors including labor market conditions, data from government agencies, retail sales, and durable goods manufacturing. There are thousands of these data points, some of which are published by private entities, and many of which are compiled and published by government agencies, such as the Bureau of Labor Statistics or the Federal Reserve System.

We devised a measurement and monitoring system based on this research and analysis and began using it in 2007. This measurement system was instrumental in showing us that conditions were deteriorating in late 2007 and that it was time to dramatically reduce risk in client portfolios before the financial crisis of 2008-2009. So far, so good.

However, what eventually became clear was that there is often a significant time lag to availability of the data. For example, when the public gets information about gross domestic product (GDP)—the broadest economic measure which measures economic growth in the aggregate—it's thirty days after the end of the last measurement period or the last quarter, and it is revised two or three times over the course of succeeding months. Therefore, the information ends up not being as useful as you think it might be. By the time you have the information, a lot may have already changed in the economy. Because of the time lag in availability of the data, we eventually had to abandon that approach.

Ultimately, we realized there is a great deal of useful information reflected in the behavior of asset prices in financial markets. By this we mean what's happening with interest rates, stock prices in different sectors of the economy, price volatility, as well as other measures. Research has shown that investors collectively are not perfectly rational, as suggested by classic economic theory. Instead, our research has shown that they overreact to good news and bad news about the economy, which in turn drives stock prices up or down. But, even though they are not perfectly rational, they are not completely bonkers. When good news is announced that would improve corporate earnings, investors bid up stock prices. They may bid them up too much (i.e., overreact), but they don't get it completely wrong. They don't bid prices down on good news.

Conversely, when there's bad news, they don't bid prices up. The term we use to describe this behavior is that investors' reaction to economic news is *directionally correct*. Investors may overreact, but they collectively react in the correct direction. What this means is there is a great deal of useful information reflected in the price behavior of financial assets in actively traded markets, and we can use that information to measure market and economic conditions. Therefore, the conditions measurement system we ultimately developed and continue to use and refine is based on the behavior of asset prices across all the relevant financial markets.

*The term we use to describe this behavior is that investors' reaction to economic news is directionally correct.*

It's important for the system to be objective, meaning there can't be any subjectivity or element of judgment driving decisions. This means it must be based entirely on hard data from reliable sources. That's crucial, for two reasons:

1. The first reason has to do with behavioral biases. We may be more aware of our innate behavioral biases than many individual investors are, but we are subject to them just like everyone else. Therefore, we can't allow investment decisions to be ruled by our emotions. We can't allow decisions to be driven by speculation about what we think might happen in the future. *Investment decisions must be based entirely on objective data, facts, and probabilistic*

*thinking.* That's the first reason the measurement system must be completely objective.

2.  The second reason is that if the measurement system is completely objective and based on hard data, it's possible to know both economic conditions and the related financial market outcomes for any period in the past. That means you can test your measurement system and any potential investment strategies you may be evaluating. For example, you can understand how an investment strategy you are considering would have behaved in certain financial market conditions that occurred in the 1960s. If you have objective data and objective rules, that means you can go back in time and see how a strategy worked in a given set of economic conditions back in that time period. That's extremely valuable when you're working to understand how investment strategies you are developing might perform in different financial market conditions.

That was the first task we undertook: develop an objective, testable measurement system for investment conditions that we continue to refine over time. Over a twenty-year period through a process of proprietary research that incorporates insights from published academic research, we developed the sophisticated investment conditions measurement system we currently use, which is based on the behavior of asset prices in actively traded financial markets.

## 2. DETERMINE THE BEST INVESTMENT ASSET CLASSES FOR EACH INVESTMENT CONDITION.

Once we created an objective way to measure conditions so that portfolios could be changed and hold different investment assets in different conditions, we needed to know which asset classes are best to hold in different conditions. The idea is that you want to hold the best investment assets for the current conditions rather than holding the same assets all the time, regardless of conditions.

When the economy is expanding and corporate profits are growing, investment conditions are favorable. Referring to our road trip metaphor, the best investment assets to hold in sunny/dry conditions are ownership interests in companies—that is, stocks. Ownership interests in companies benefit from favorable conditions because a growing economy and growing corporate profits drive stock prices up. Remember, a lemonade stand that makes $200 is more valuable than the same lemonade stand making $100. It is the process of growing profits that increases stock prices.

As we discussed earlier, the Standard Model regards stocks as a risky investment, but the reality is that when investment conditions are favorable, it's not risky to hold stocks, just as it's not risky to drive seventy-five miles an hour when the road is dry.

When conditions change, however, meaning the economy is beginning to slow or slide into recession, the short-term impact on company earnings is great. For example, in a garden-variety recession, total corporate profits often decline on a short-term basis by 50 percent. In the recession of 2008, corporate profits declined by 100 percent. Even though the decline in corporate profits is a short-term phenomenon and profits will recover when the economy begins growing again, we know that stock prices drop dramatically with a decline in profits. Therefore, when these conditions begin to develop, stocks become a very risky asset. In these conditions, you don't want to hold them in your portfolio.

However, there are investment assets that have historically benefited from unfavorable investment conditions. When conditions are unfavorable, US treasury bonds, often referred to as "the safest asset on the planet," can have very nice gains. They not only protect capital, but historically have gained in value because investors flee to these types of safe assets in unfavorable conditions, thereby driving prices up. That's called the "flight to safety." Therefore, when conditions are very unfavorable, it makes sense to hold assets like US government bonds that defend capital and have the potential for gains instead of stocks.

There is a great deal more to it than can be covered in this brief overview. We have done a tremendous amount of research on how all the different asset classes that are traded in financial markets have behaved historically in different investment conditions. Because we have an objective data-driven measurement system and ninety years of data on financial market conditions and outcomes, we can look back to any period in history and see how different asset classes performed in different investment conditions.

We have previously made the point that the traditional, generic bond allocations most investors follow in implementing the Standard Model will fare poorly in the future interest rate environment. This is because standard bond allocations typically "buy and hold" a broad cross-section of bond categories that remains unchanged regardless of conditions. However, because different types of bonds respond differently to changing business cycle conditions, active management of bond holdings in the portfolio is imperative.

In the bond arena, there are US government bonds, investment grade corporate bonds, and below-investment grade bonds, otherwise known as high-yield bonds, which are issued by large companies that are less credit-worthy than average. These are all different investment assets and have different characteristics in terms of how they respond to different conditions. For example, Treasury bonds and high-yield bonds are both "bonds." However, Treasury bonds typically do well when investment conditions are unfavorable, and high-yield bonds provide gains and attractive interest payments when conditions are favorable. Therefore, it makes sense to hold Treasury and high-yield bonds in the portfolio at different times, depending on investment conditions. As we said, the idea is to hold the best investment assets for the current conditions rather than the same assets all the time regardless of conditions.

## 3. DESIGN INVESTMENT STRATEGIES AND RELATED TRADING RULES.

Once you can measure conditions and know which investment assets you should hold for different conditions, you can design investment strategies with different characteristics to meet different needs. In other words, for a given set of financial market conditions, what asset class investments should we hold and what are the rules that are going to tell you when it's time to change?

To design an investment strategy, you need to evaluate and balance outcomes across four different dimensions which are inherently conflicting. Those dimensions are:

1. investment return,

2. risk,

3. trading frequency, and

4. tracking difference.

When we say the dimensions are inherently conflicting, we mean it's impossible to optimize across all four dimensions. Improving one dimension will usually mean that one of the other dimensions suffers. For example, we may be able to design a strategy that produces a higher return, but the tradeoff is that it requires more trading in client accounts, or larger periodic drawdowns (higher risk) than we target.

We have created several investment strategies which are designed to cover most client situations. Each of these strategies have a different combination of these attributes: different potential investment return, different level of risk, different trading frequency, and different worse-case tracking differences. These are all attributes that we can analyze, quantify, and explain to clients, so they know what to expect and can decide which strategy makes the most sense for them.

## Investment Return

Investment returns are what all investors seek from their portfolio. In one sense, the idea is self-explanatory and there is no need to belabor the point. Obviously, a primary consideration in designing an investment strategy is the potential investment return. However, here is the key question to answer: Over what period are we measuring investment returns? As we have discussed, common sense and our behavioral biases, particularly the recency bias, often lead us to the wrong conclusion in evaluating investment strategies.

A point we have made repeatedly throughout this book is that the only investment returns that matter for long-term investors are those earned over the complete business cycle. If you suffer large financial losses in your portfolio, it may take years to recover. Many investors never recover. Therefore, when designing investment strategies, the relevant period for measuring investment returns is the complete business cycle.

## Risk

As a matter of common sense, a layperson might say that you really don't need to know anything more than the investment return for a given strategy. However, the real question is: How much risk do you have to take to generate that return? If you earned a 10 percent return but had to risk losing 75 percent of your money, most people would say that wasn't a very good investment decision.

The risk measurement method we favor is called "drawdown," which measures from the high-water mark of your portfolio to the lowest value before the portfolio begins to grow again. During unfavorable conditions, it is inevitable that portfolios will give back some of the ground you'd previously gained. *Drawdown* is the amount of ground you had to give up.

Drawdown is useful for two reasons:

1.  It matters in determining portfolio outcomes. If you minimize drawdown, your portfolio starts its growth from a higher value when the difficult period ends. Therefore, you get a better portfolio outcome in the long term. We discussed this in chapter 2 when we looked at the performance of low-volatility stocks versus the S&P 500. Low-volatility stocks were behind 78 percent of the time but produced a nearly three-times better outcome over two business cycles. This was because of lower drawdowns. Low volatility did a better job minimizing losses during the bad times, and so started from a higher value during the good times. Drawdown is critically important in determining portfolio outcome.

2.  It reflects how investors experience risk. Even long-term investors "anchor" on the highest value they have achieved

in their portfolio. For example, they may say, "I used to have a million-dollar portfolio and now it's down to $700,000." That's an emotional issue and it's the reality of how individual investors experience risk. The larger the drawdown, the greater the emotional angst for the individual investor.

For both reasons, it's important to measure and minimize drawdown: to get a better portfolio outcome and to reduce emotional angst for investors.

## Trading Frequency

Because we measure conditions daily, it is technically possible for us to design investment strategies that would change the portfolio every day and potentially generate higher returns. But, that's a lot of trading and we view a high volume of trading as undesirable for client portfolios.

As we design potential strategies, we calculate two measures of trading frequency: the average number of trades per year, and the maximum number of trades per year. For example, we recently implemented improvements to one of our investment strategies. The improvements were based on incorporating more detailed data in our conditions measurement system, plus some minor changes in the related trading rules. The result was better returns over the complete business cycle, less drawdown risk, but slightly higher trading frequency.

The previous versions of the strategy traded an average of two times per year, with an expected maximum of four trades per year. The improved strategy is expected to trade an average of three times per year, with a maximum of six trades per year. In this case, we believed the better investment returns with less risk were worth the disadvantage of a few additional potential trades per year in client accounts. However, there is always a trade-off because it's impossible to achieve the optimum result across each of the four measures. If you improve one element, it's likely there will be a tradeoff in one or more of the other attributes.

## Tracking Difference

Tracking difference relates to behavioral biases, particularly the recency bias. Because the media is constantly reporting the daily outcome of financial markets, most investors have some idea what an average portfolio outcome might be on a short-term basis. Therefore, the tendency is to compare the short-term results in their portfolio to how they perceive financial markets performed during the same period. If their portfolio results are less on a short-term basis than their mental benchmark, investors' inherent recency bias can sometimes become an issue. Even though we have demonstrated that these short-term differences are irrelevant to the ultimate outcome in the portfolio, nonetheless, recency bias is hard-wired in all investors. Because this is how individual investors tend to think about the problem, it is important for us to be aware of the issue so that we can manage expectations. We always seek to educate investors to help them understand that, from time-to-time, there will be differences in their portfolio performance versus mental benchmarks. We also try to explain how much those differences might be, how long they will last, and that they are expected as a normal part of the process of getting a better wealth outcome.

Therefore, as we design and evaluate potential investment strategies, we use a measure called "tracking difference." This is a measure of how much, if any, an investment strategy may lag the stock market or the common 60 percent stocks/40 percent bonds passive portfolio on a short-term basis. The question our tracking difference measurement answers is: How much does the strategy vary from the benchmark, by what percentage, and how often does it happen? Obviously, there will be times during the short term when the strategy outcome is better than the benchmark, but we don't bother to measure those instances. There is no behavioral bias associated with tracking better than the market at any point in time.

Negative tracking difference (i.e., tracking worse than the benchmark in the short term) can become an issue for some investors because of the recency bias. It's impossible to design a strategy that has the best returns, the lowest risk, the least amount of trading, and completely avoid negative tracking difference. What you will find is that you can design strategies which increase your return, but the tradeoff is greater drawdown or higher periodic risk. You can design a strategy that will improve your return but will require you to trade more frequently, or you may be able to design a strategy that produces much better returns over the complete business cycle but also produces a lot of negative tracking difference. Remember the example of the low volatility strategy. It produced much better returns than the S&P 500 with less risk, but lagged the S&P 500 78 percent of the time. That's a lot of negative tracking difference for people to tolerate.

These are the measurement dimensions we use to shape our investment strategies. Each strategy we design has a different potential investment return, a different level of risk, a different level of trading frequency, as well as a different potential tracking difference. These dimensions and the tradeoffs between the dimensions can be analyzed to help decide which strategy makes the most sense for any investor.

## 4. MONITOR AND REPORT INVESTMENT CONDITIONS DAILY.

We believe it's necessary to measure conditions in financial markets on a daily basis because things can change pretty quickly. If you measure monthly or quarterly, you will likely find yourself behind the curve in responding to developments in financial markets.

When you measure daily and you see things develop over a period of time, you can begin to discern that things are changing. In financial markets, road conditions do not instantly become icy; you will notice that it's getting colder and maybe you're starting to see some snow flurries. Because you are paying attention every day and seeing conditions over time, you know change is coming.

Snow flurries, for example, could be volatility in financial markets. Increased market volatility indicates nervousness on the part of investors. Increasing volatility often occurs when investors are collectively responding to an important change in the economy that may impact corporate earnings.

To help us track these changes, we designed technology systems to collect data from the day's events. By two o'clock each morning, we have a new set of data which reflects the most recent conditions in financial markets. In addition, we have created a database that reflects daily investment conditions going back to the late 1920s. This allows us to understand not only current conditions, but what the outcome of those conditions has been at any time in the past. We report a summary of this information via weekly email newsletter to all our clients. We tell them what's going on, what happened this week, what investment conditions currently are, any concerns we have about developing conditions, and therefore how their portfolios are currently invested.

## 5. IMPLEMENT AND MAINTAIN A TECHNOLOGY PLATFORM THAT SUPPORTS ACTIVE MANAGEMENT.

Once we could measure conditions and design strategies based on the daily monitoring of conditions, we needed a technology solution that gave us the capability to manage changes in client portfolios. What happens if you are managing thousands of client accounts, and conditions change requiring changes in all portfolios in just a matter of hours? It's simply impossible to address the problem by trading each account individually, one by one. Therefore, it was critical to implement technology that enables the management of thousands of accounts representing different combinations of investment strategies.

## 6. MANAGE PORTFOLIOS BASED ON PRE-DEFINED, OBJECTIVE TRADING RULES.

It's important to manage investment portfolios based on predefined, objective trading rules. It's essential to have hard and fast rules that specify a particular action that must be taken when certain conditions occur. This removes judgment and bias from the decision. This is what we call a "100 percent rules-based approach."

This is important, for a couple of reasons. As we said previously, emotion is the enemy when change is occurring in financial markets. Your strategy needs to be objective. That's the benefit of having predefined rules and probabilistic thinking: in any given condition, you know exactly what action is required. You know this because you have tested it in different market conditions and it has the highest likelihood of producing better portfolio outcomes. For example, in condition A, this asset gets sold, and that asset gets bought. This is what trading rules do.

It's important to note that we don't regard these strategies as being "predictive" in any sense of the word. We have no idea what will happen tomorrow, next week, next month, etc., and neither does anyone else. *Instead, better investing is based on probabilistic thinking.* For example, it may be possible to know from our data that when a particular set of investment conditions has existed in the past, 80 percent of the time it was the prelude to large losses, and, therefore, based on probabilistic thinking, it makes sense to reduce risk in those conditions.

## 7. HOLD LOW-COST, HIGHLY-LIQUID ASSET CLASS INVESTMENTS (E.G., ETFs).

The best way to implement the strategies described in this book is to hold low-cost, highly liquid asset class investments, specifically exchange traded funds (ETFs). ETFs are a type of investment asset that developed in the late 1990s.

> "An ETF is a marketable security that tracks an index, a commodity, bonds, or a basket of assets like an index fund. Unlike mutual funds, an ETF trades like a common stock on a stock exchange. ETFs experience price changes throughout the day as they are bought and sold. ETFs typically have higher daily liquidity and lower fees than do mutual fund shares, making them an attractive alternative for individual investors."[52]

---

52  Definition of Exchange Traded Fund, *Investopedia*. Available at https://www.investopedia.com/terms/e/etf.asp

ETFs are typically not actively managed, so there's no investment manager making decisions about what stocks they're going to hold and charging fees for that service. ETFs are designed to track, for example, the S&P 500, the Russell 2000, the Midcap 600, or the US Treasury twenty-year duration and greater index. It owns the underlying assets and then divides ownership of those assets into shares.

ETFs deliver pure asset class exposure. *This is important because the asset class you hold in a given condition determines your outcome.* Earlier we made the point that research has shown that when broad diversification is employed, 90–100 percent of the risk and return outcome of the portfolio is determined by asset class allocation, and virtually none of the outcome is determined by which securities you hold within each asset class. ETFs are the perfect instruments to apply this insight because they represent pure asset class exposure and don't have extra fees for security selection that don't add value to the portfolio.

Additionally, ETFs are typically highly liquid and can be traded instantly. They're also extremely low cost because they are simple financial instruments designed to track a published index. There's typically no active investment manager picking stocks and charging extra fees for that work. The decision about what securities to hold has already been made. This makes ETFs very low cost and the preferred vehicle to implement the strategy we've presented in this book.

## 8. MAINTAIN THE DISCIPLINE, COMMITMENT, AND READINESS TO ACT EVERY DAY.

Finally, it is critical to have the discipline, commitment and readiness to act every day as needed. If our investment strategies have been designed properly, trading (i.e., changing portfolios) will be relatively infrequent. Nonetheless, to implement active management of portfolio risk, it is necessary to be prepared every day to make changes in portfolios, even though most of the time, no changes will be required. However, when changes are necessary, it is critical to be ready to act.

# CONCLUSION

*In review, this book is the product of our efforts* to solve for
ourselves the same problem clients have repeatedly expressed to us:
What is the best way to manage our accumulated wealth to ensure
that we have enough for what matters? The common concern we
hear is: Will we have enough? If you don't like the answer, you want
to know what you can do about it.

If your objective is to improve the odds of having enough, or
if you see the benefit beyond yourself of creating more for what
matters, by far the highest-impact strategy available is to become a
better investor. This was the problem we set out to solve for ourselves
nearly twenty years ago. Ultimately, we decided to write this book
because what we'd learned was so important.

Our focus was to help individual investors understand the
arguments for a better alternative to the standard portfolio management orthodoxy advocated by the investment advice industry. A
better wealth outcome means: the portfolio supports higher withdrawals before being exhausted, or you have greater ending portfolio
wealth with less risk.

We have written at length about the Standard Model. It is not a bad solution to the individual investment problem. In fact, it has many advantages:

- It has been shown to consistently produce better outcomes than those achieved by individual investors acting on their own.

- It provides important discipline for the investment process.

- It requires broad diversification to reduce individual firm and security risk.

- It assumes that asset class allocation is the most important determinant of portfolio risk and return rather than security selection. Research has shown that asset allocation determines between 90 percent to 100 percent of portfolio return and risk.

While the Standard Model is a good solution compared to what individual investors typically achieve on their own, that does not mean it's the best solution to the retirement portfolio problem. In fact, we would say it is seriously dated. We part company with the Standard Model in one key area that has major implications for portfolio management: the assumed constancy of the risk/return relationship of asset classes. The Standard Model assumes that the risk/return relationship of asset classes is constant. However, our research has shown this is not true. Instead, the risk/return relationship varies considerably for each asset class based on investment conditions.

The assumption of the constancy of the risk/return relationship turns out to have significant implications for portfolio management. Because the Standard Model assumes that risk/return is constant, it takes a passive approach to managing the asset class composition of the portfolio. It does this by prescribing a static, unchanging asset class allocation. The Standard Model requires that portfolio allocations should always remain the same except when there has been a major change in the investor's personal situation, tolerance for risk or need for growth.

*However, if asset class risk/return is not constant and instead varies depending on conditions, and if asset allocation determines nearly all portfolio risk and return, then the Standard Model can be significantly improved by actively managing the asset class composition of the portfolio.* This means the portfolio should change as conditions change. For example, rather than a constant 60/40 percent allocation between stocks and bonds regardless of conditions, portfolios should hold a higher percentage of stocks when conditions are favorable for that asset class, and a lower percentage or even no stocks when conditions are unfavorable.

Nearly twenty years after we began a concerted effort to become better investors, we can summarize what we have learned in three principles:

1. If you want a better result, you have to do something different. It should be obvious that following the Standard Model will yield the standard results. However, our objective was to apply the insights from leading academic research and our own research to improve returns and reduce risk in comparison to the Standard Model.

2. Taking a different approach requires thinking differently about the problem. Sometimes a better investment approach may even be counterintuitive and contrary to our common-sense instincts in the short-term. The paradox of better investing is that the solution is partly technical and partly behavioral. Granted, there are some technical improvements that must be developed and mastered.

However, the primary reason it's hard for many people to become better investors is that our common-sense beliefs about investing often lead us astray. The greatest obstacle to becoming a better investor is the six inches between our ears.

3.   The outcome is worth it. We have already made the point that the highest impact strategy for changing wealth outcomes is becoming a better investor. We believe the ideas summarized in this book can be transformational for retirement portfolios.

To help you achieve your goals, we have advocated a markedly different approach than the standard approach recommended by the investment advice industry. We believe active rather than passive management of portfolio asset allocation is a better approach to the problem.

Wherever you are on your investment journey, we hope you will find the road trip metaphor useful in thinking about how to approach the problem. It rarely makes sense to drive the same speed for your entire trip. Instead when road conditions are favorable, you should drive fast because it's not risky in those conditions. But when the roads are icy and a winter storm threatens, the risk of crashing has increased significantly. When that happens, it makes sense to slow down or even pull off the road.

There are many other illustrations we could use. Physicians prescribe patient treatment based on the evidence. As the symptoms change, treatment may change. In football, quarterbacks read the defense and often make changes at the line of scrimmage based on what they see. Baseball teams change their defensive alignment based on the tendencies of the hitter. As an avid golfer, Tom selects his club and type of shot based on the distance to the hole, wind, and other conditions. These are all examples of changing what we do based on the conditions we encounter.

We acknowledge that it can be difficult to find a financial advisor who embraces these ideas and who has the experience, research, and technology to apply them on your behalf. But that is changing. The most important thing is to become an informed purchaser and know what you want and expect from your advisor.

There is always a business cycle with both expansions and recessions. Controlling losses matters far more than getting all the gains. You will finish far ahead by capturing your fair share of the gains while avoiding large losses. That is the key to having more for what matters and is the essence of *Transformational Investing*.